Terence Conran
Making Modern Britain

Deyan Sudjic

**the
DESIGN
MUSEUM**

Contents

Introduction	6
An education in the arts and crafts	22
Working for other people	62
Working for himself	86
You are what you eat	116
Tastemaking	144
The big bang	174
Design and culture	192
Epilogue	226

Introduction

Terence Conran was a lifelong collector. He kept an album of pressed flowers on a shelf by his desk at his country home at Barton Court until the day that he died, aged eighty-eight. It was about the size of a hymn book, packed full of faded dandelions, thistles and desiccated wildflowers. There is no way of telling if this is actually the book that he had put together himself at his Hampshire prep school aged ten, during the course of a single summer collecting wildflowers from the fields and hedgerows around Old Shepherd's Farm, the house in which he lived during most of the Second World War. To keep the petals from turning brown, he had to dry and then immediately press the flowers between two sheets of absorbent paper. Each specimen is carefully annotated in pencil in a childish script that bears no recognisable relationship to his handwriting as an adult. Perhaps this album is his own work, or maybe it is in itself another kind of collector's piece, acquired later for its aesthetic quality rather than as a reminder of his own childhood.

While he was still at prep school, Terence also started collecting moths and butterflies. This was a more demanding process than pressing flowers. To present-day sensibilities, it may seem a macabre enthusiasm, but at the time entomology was still considered an innocent-enough pastime. It involved him trapping his prey in a delicate butterfly net, and killing it before the victim could become distressed enough to damage its wings in the struggle to be free. One recommended method was to squeeze the thorax. A jar, lined with a layer of plaster of Paris saturated with chloroform or ethyl acetate, worked just as well. Each catch would be handled with soft cotton gloves to avoid damaging the fragile scales, and then stored in an envelope. When enough specimens had been gathered, the next step was impaling each butterfly, moth or beetle on a needle, then arranging them in intricate patterns on a board and finally placing them in glass-fronted cases. He kept one in his study.

In later life, at Barton Court, Terence installed a flock of blue Bugatti vintage toy pedal cars of varying sizes pinned like wingless butterflies to the wall of a corridor in the Berkshire house that he had bought in 1971. Barton Court is an eighteenth-century house with nineteenth-century additions built of a warm red,

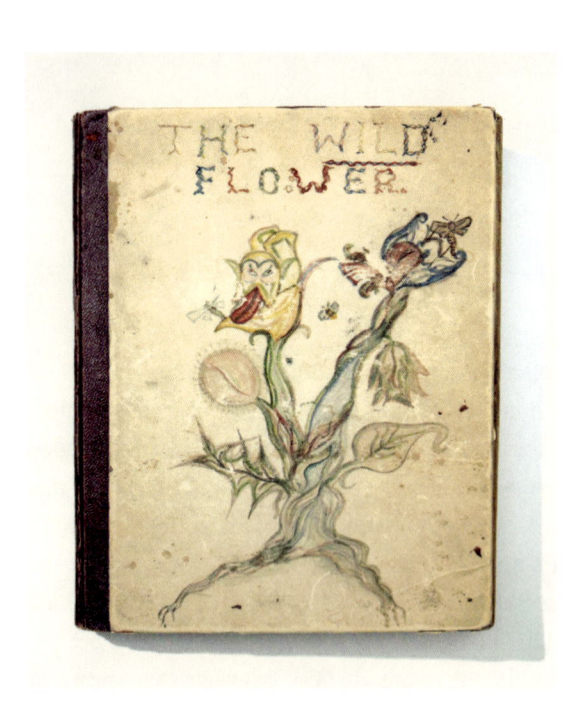

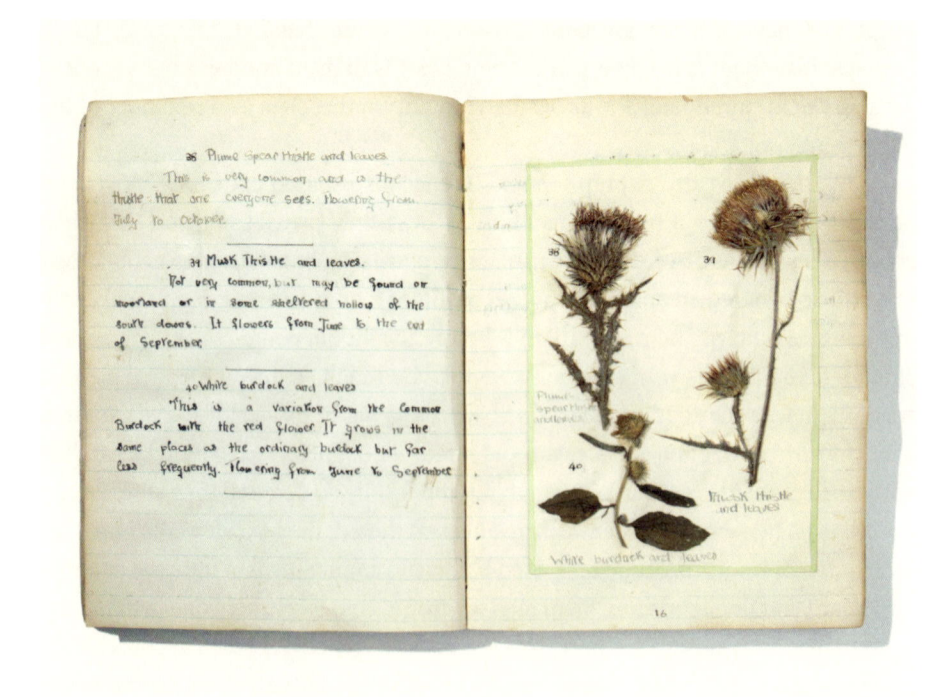

Terence's enthusiasm for collecting began with pressing wildflowers. He kept this book of specimens in his office, alongside a case of butterflies, which were another schoolboy passion

TERENCE CONRAN   MAKING MODERN BRITAIN

INTRODUCTION

Barton Court, Terence's Berkshire home since 1971. He replanned the approach to the house so that visitors arrived through the generously scaled new kitchen, rather than the formal front door

almost orange, brick. It was one of the first fruits of the wealth that came from his most important success: the Habitat furniture business. Unlike the flowers and moths that he had spent so much time on as a child, he acquired the Bugatti collection ready-made as a single lot. The pedal cars were beautiful to look at, even though some of them were a little battered and showed traces of their use by previous, much younger and less careful owners.

Some collectors seek to make a pattern out of the items that they acquire, or like jigsaw puzzlers set out to complete a picture by locating every piece of a set. Terence didn't have the patience to be that kind of a collector. Some try to document the evolution of a species, from biscuit tins to plovers' eggs. Others simply accumulate material. Sigmund Freud amassed hundreds of pieces of classical sculpture in the course of his career, and in 1938 shipped them from his consulting room in Vienna to London, having photographed them in place, so that they could be reassembled in an identical sequence while he was in exile in Hampstead. Freud touched on the psychology of collecting in his writing. He regarded it as a form of control. The writer Orhan Pamuk portrayed the range of impulses behind collecting in his novel *The Museum of Innocence*, as both a consolation and a signal of spiritual distress.

The connecting thread in Terence's collecting impulses was certainly design. He was both a collector and a designer. They are two activities that, while they are not the same, have some things in common. Collecting can be understood as a reflection of the impulse to find order, which is the underlying motivation of the designer. Collecting is also an accumulation of ideas, motifs and components, without necessarily having a specific purpose, that might eventually turn out to be useful. And that can be described as an essential part of the design process too.

TERENCE CONRAN   MAKING MODERN BRITAIN

INTRODUCTION

Terence's office on the first floor of Barton Court was lined with open shelves. The top layer was devoted to working models for his own furniture designs and other pieces manufactured by Benchmark, which is based on the estate. The next shelf down was for his collection of doll's-house-scale miniature furniture. His books, from student texts to treatises on industrial design and Viennese modernist interiors, were in easy reach on the lower shelves

Terence acquired his Bugatti pedal cars, pinned like wingless butterflies to the wall, as a ready-made collection

INTRODUCTION

If collecting was one essential aspect of Terence's early years that would offer clues to the direction his life would take, the other was an enduring fascination with making. For Terence's eightieth birthday, Benchmark, the furniture workshop he established with Sean Sutcliffe (a graduate of John Makepeace's School for Craftsmen in Wood), and based in what had once been farm buildings in the grounds of Barton Court, made him a simple but handsome wooden cabinet. It was fitted out with an intricate nest of compartments to accommodate a full set of woodworking hand tools that included an assortment of chisels of various sizes, saws and hammers, planes, set-squares and spirit levels, each of them carefully selected by one of the workshop's skilled craftsmen to be the best of its kind – which was usually not the most expensive example available, but one which had been tested in use. The tools themselves have been shaped by the kind of unselfconscious utility that always appealed to Terence. These are artefacts that have been created with a sense of purpose, to carry out a task, rather than to impress or flatter their owner. He kept the cabinet in his office at home, another ready-made collection, and a poignant reminder of the skills that he had started to learn at school seventy years earlier, even as the physical drawbacks of ageing kept him from using its contents. 'The best toy I ever had,' Terence once said, 'was a woodworking set. It included a hammer, a gimlet, a bag of nails and some bits of wood.' While he was growing up, he got to know all about the uses of a spokeshave – the best way to shape a piece of wood before the invention of power tools. He could build a wood-fired kiln. He knew how to 'pug' clay, which is to say, how to use his hands to work all the air bubbles out of the material to prepare it to make a flowerpot, which he did on a foot-powered potter's wheel. One of Terence's mantras was that until a designer knew how to make what they had designed, they could not claim to have actually designed it.

Collecting, making and food were the three shared enthusiasms that drew Terence close to the sculptor Eduardo Paolozzi, perhaps the most influential figure in his early life aside from his mother Christina and his sister Priscilla. Paolozzi and Terence were both makers, and it was that passion that underpinned their working relationship. Paolozzi was his tutor at the Central School of Arts and Crafts in London, and a great accumulator of toys, propellers, magazines and newspapers as the source of an important aspect of his art, as well as an artist ready to work with his own hands. Paolozzi shared with Terence the kitchen skills he had learned from his Italian parents. At Barton Court, Terence kept one of the terracotta tile reliefs that had been shown at the Mayor Gallery's Paolozzi exhibition in 1949, along with the Anthony Caro table piece that the sculptor gave him to mark the closure of Garage, the art gallery in Covent Garden that Terence had funded for

TERENCE CONRAN   MAKING MODERN BRITAIN

The woodworkers of Benchmark, based at
Barton Court, reflect a continuing passion
for skill

Anthony Caro's table piece was a gift to mark the closing of the Garage gallery in 1975

Terracotta tile by Eduardo Paolozzi, acquired in 1949

Benchmark celebrated Terence's eightieth birthday with a carefully chosen collection of woodworking tools

two years in the 1970s. The tile shows the marks of nails and other objects that have been pressed into it, like archaeological traces. The pieces of Paolozzi's work that Terence liked best were the ones that showed the traces of his hands, and these tended to be from the sculptor's earlier days.

Terence began his career as a designer in 1949, leaving the Central School without a diploma aged seventeen, having completed just two of the three years of a course in textile design. However, it did not take him long to make a mark. By the time he was twenty-six he had already started his own design studio and a showroom, along with a workshop to make furniture, opened five restaurants,

When he was just twenty years old, Terence started his own business, working on projects that ranged from designing and making furniture to graphics, textiles and even clothing

launched a fabric business with his second wife, Shirley, and written his first book. He had exhibited his work at Simpson department store in Piccadilly, art directed a magazine and printed textiles for Matisse, although the artist never knew of his existence.

Terence's rapid accumulation of projects and businesses was a reflection of his driven energy, a quality that would one day attract the attention of London's financiers. They gave him the chance to collect businesses in the financial boom of the 1980s. In thirty years, he went from exhibiting his work in an artist's studio on Fitzroy Street alongside Paolozzi, Ben Nicholson and Victor Pasmore to becoming the chairman of a £1.8 billion, publicly listed company with tens of thousands of employees. His headquarters was in the Heal's Building, on the other side of Tottenham Court Road from the long-demolished studio on Fitzroy Street. Before the decade was over, Terence had also acquired an eleven-acre development site in London's Docklands, and started the Design Museum, a publishing company and an architectural practice. He bought Richard Shops and British Home Stores, Mothercare, Heal's and Blazer. But he would soon leave his retail group, Storehouse, and see the Butler's Wharf development forced into bankruptcy when the property market turned from boom to bust, and his bank called in its loan. When he stepped away from running Storehouse, Terence embarked on yet another phase of his career – opening restaurant after restaurant, a collection in itself.

The trajectory of Terence's own life intersected with that of contemporary Britain – sometimes echoing it, sometimes shaping it. In his paint-splattered overalls, he had a walk-on part as a teenage technician at the Festival of Britain, racing to finish the display in time for the opening. He was certainly part of the hedonistic explosion of affluence in the 1960s, designing Mary Quant's shop in Knightsbridge and opening Habitat. In 1973 he opened his largest Habitat store under a cinema on the King's Road just as the then prime minister Edward Heath took on Britain's striking coalminers. Terence had to use candles to light the shop during the three-day weeks of rolling power cuts, a national emergency that coincided with an IRA bombing campaign targeting London.

In the 1980s, Terence was politically left-leaning and politely refused a dinner invitation to Downing Street during the Falklands War; however, he also developed

Mary Quant's shop on Knightsbridge Green opened in 1959. A double-height space was formed by opening up the basement. Customers descended by way of a mezzanine. Pale grey and white finishes, hardwoods and leather formed a discreet setting for Quant's colourful clothes

INTRODUCTION

The first Habitat store opened on London's Fulham Road in 1964. It was an attempt to do for the home what Mary Quant had done for fashion

a working relationship with Margaret Thatcher, who approved his knighthood and opened the Design Museum in 1989. In the same decade he became the face of corporate financial engineering, as the figurehead for contested takeovers. Ralph Halpern and Terence posed together for an advertising campaign when Halpern was bidding to buy the Debenhams department store chain. They were well-enough known to be shown seated in director's chairs with their backs to their audience. In the 1990s, Terence hosted Tony Blair's dinner with Bill Clinton at Le Pont de la Tour, the restaurant that he owned by Tower Bridge.

* * *

I first met Terence in 1977. He was at Trelowarren House, on the Lizard Peninsula, giving a talk to the Cornwall Crafts Association in memory of its founder Wyndham Gooden, former professor of textiles at the Royal College of Art, who had been his friend and an early supporter.

I lived for a time in a room in a palatial stucco-fronted house in Saint Andrew's Place in the southeast corner of Regent's Park that Terence once leased from the Crown Estate and had used as the setting for some of the most atmospheric photographs in the Habitat catalogue. Terence's eldest son Sebastian was letting rooms to fellow student friends from the Central School. Sebastian would shortly follow in the family tradition and leave the school before graduating. In his case it was to work with the Clash, having booked the Sex Pistols in 1976 for a memorable early performance at the Central School.

Terence was a supporter of *Blueprint*, the magazine that I edited, though it was Caroline Conran, his third wife, who invested in it personally. He recommended me to the New Millennium Experience Company as one of two candidates for the

Despite his doubts about Conservative policies, Margaret Thatcher, seen here with Stuart Mosscrop (the architect who led the team master planning Butler's Wharf), was an important supporter, both in Terence's business activities in the 1980s, and in setting up the Design Museum

role of creative director of the Dome (now the O2 Arena). Luckily for me they selected Stephen Bayley – who had been my predecessor-but-three as director of the Design Museum – for the job.

To mark Terence's eightieth birthday, I worked with Stafford Cliff, the designer of the most original editions of the Habitat catalogue, to stage a retrospective exhibition of his work at the Design Museum at its former site at Shad Thames. All of which is to say that there are moments in Terence's long and eventful career in which I have been something more than a bystander.

This book is an account of Terence's life and work. For a life as full as Terence's, a chronological account risks sounding like a breathless commentary at a racetrack. Instead, I have explored seven themes in his life, from food to business, that help to define his complex character. He was perhaps a collector of careers: a maker, a designer, a manufacturer, a retailer and a restaurateur. And above all, a tastemaker.

For most of the second half of the twentieth century, Terence offered a glimpse of a way of life that many of his fellow Britons were keen to share vicariously and which in time reached shops in Japan and Korea, France and Holland, as well as restaurants in America and Sweden. He, more than anyone, shaped the culture of everyday life in Britain for more than four decades. He was also a collector of people. Those who became close to him in work or in life, or both, were also attracted by that way of life he seemed to represent. Like most successful people, he knew how to make use of the power of that attraction.

Inevitably the fashionable in time becomes the formerly fashionable. Terence has been seen through both lenses, yet he still emerges as a figure of more than transient significance. To get to know Terence is to understand a lot about the texture of contemporary life in this country.

An education in the
arts and crafts

TERENCE CONRAN   MAKING MODERN BRITAIN

Terence Orby Conran was born on 4 October 1931. His father, Rupert Conran, had been born in Cape Town, South Africa, when Rupert's parents were en route from Australia to Britain. His mother, Christina Halstead, was born in Chelsea but grew up in Chichester. Terence's parents moved from a terraced house in Kensington to a villa in Esher while his mother was pregnant with him. His first, indistinct memory as a child was of lying in the garden of his parents' new home, looking up at an apple tree and seeing the sun shining through its leaves. His sister Priscilla was born five years later. The family subsequently moved to a flat in a mansion block off the Finchley Road in North London.

One of the recurring themes of Terence's life was his discontent with what he saw as the limitations of suburban life; this he shared with many members of his generation of the comfortable, well-educated middle classes. From the way that he spoke, sometimes dismissively, about Esher, you sensed that if Terence could have had the choice, he would have preferred to grow up as the child of a market porter in Les Halles, a gardener in Dorset or an artist in Bloomsbury, rather than the son of a commodity trader who caught the train to Waterloo every morning.

Rupert Conran was supportive of his son. He coached him at rugby. He helped him to establish his business, eventually transferring the ownership of the shell of his own gum-importing firm, Conran and Co., to Terence, and introducing him to his personal accountant to audit his books. He showed signs of creativity himself, drawing for pleasure in pen and Indian ink.

But Terence's world was not the same as his father's. He credited his mother with giving him the first glimpses of a life beyond Esher, in which how things looked and what they meant really mattered. It was his mother who took Terence and his sister Priscilla – a close confidante throughout his life – to exhibitions at the Royal Academy, to the occasional exotic Chinese meal in 1940s Soho, and to Heal's – the store that the Heal family had opened on Tottenham Court Road to sell well-made Arts and Crafts furniture.

He believed it was her decision to send him to Bryanston, rather than Eton, more than it was his father's. Terence suggested that his mother even helped him when he started the Orrery restaurant in 1954 by coming in occasionally to do the

Rupert Conran and Christina Halstead on their wedding day, 22 December 1928, in London

Priscilla Conran grew up to share her brother's entrepreneurial instincts

washing up. She found him his first room in London in his student days, when it became obvious that he could no longer commute from Hampshire to his classes at the Central School of Arts and Crafts. In the months before her early death aged sixty-five, he went through the pain of being at her bedside as she told him that she was not ready to die. She said that she wanted to live long enough to see what her children were able to achieve. Terence was much less warm about his father, whom he believed was a disappointed, unfulfilled and sometimes difficult man.

Just as he was uneasy about having been born in Esher, Terence had an equally complicated relationship with class. He talked about it as if he wanted both to belong, and not to belong. Terence's parents maintained a relatively comfortable way of life; he had a nanny, and there was a family car. His father had the resources to set him up with a guaranteed overdraft of £300 in 1955. But Terence's mother had grown up in her grandmother's house in Chichester with a cook and four other servants. Terence thought that, as a result, she always felt a little awkward at taking too much interest in cooking on her own account. His paternal grandmother's family, the Slopers, had once been affluent enough to own a Reynolds portrait and pieces of Jacobean glass. In earlier centuries, the Slopers administered India and commissioned the building of substantial country houses.

Terence saw himself as part of a generation that had lost that wealth and status. It freed him from membership of a class within which he did not feel comfortable. He talked about his political ambivalence in sending his children to the same private schools he attended. At the same time, he had a nuanced fascination with his family history.

Conran is an Irish name, but Terence's family connection with Australia goes back to the 1840s, when Lewis Charles Conran moved from Suffolk to what would become the Australian state of Victoria. His grandson, Bernard Hamilton Conran, Terence's grandfather, was born in Queensland in 1864. Succeeding generations of the family spent extended periods of time back in Britain. Bernard Conran married Terence's grandmother, Charlotte Orby Sloper from Stow-on-the-Wold, in St Giles Church, Westminster, in 1905. He made enough money to allow him to move to Britain permanently, where he prospered as a stockbroker. They lived for a time in a flat in Marylebone's Bickenhall Mansions, with two servants and a nursemaid for Rupert's young sister, Evelyn.

Terence's middle name, Orby, is an inheritance from his paternal grandmother, Charlotte. It was the name that his mother called him. Terence in turn gave it to his eldest son, Sebastian, as his middle name, suggesting a certain respect for family history. But to judge by some of the items in the collection of memorabilia that Terence acquired over the years, he had an ambivalent view of his family's past.

He took wry pleasure in a letter from Lord Chief Justice Sir John Willis in 1752 to William Sloper. Willis called Terence's ancestor, his new son-in-law, 'villainous' for having eloped with his daughter, Jane, and cut them off 'without a farthing'.[1] The displeasure of the lord chief justice, no paragon of virtue himself, did Sloper's career no harm. He became commander-in-chief of British forces in India, but was sent home for the misappropriation of funds. He was suspected of using public money to support his numerous dependents, legitimate and otherwise.

After boarding school, Rupert Conran briefly joined the army himself, but left it to become a commodity trader, dealing first in coffee, then rubber. Subsequently, he set up his own business, Conran and Co., to import gum copal, the resin used to make paints and varnishes, from Central Africa. Rupert was twenty-six years old when Terence was born. Terence's mother, orphaned at twelve, had worked in a solicitor's office in London before she married.

Terence remembers his parents' homes as being furnished with what he called blocky, modern furniture set off with older antiques, and Dutch flower paintings in elaborately ornate gilt frames that were reminders of earlier generations of

Conrans, Halsteads and Slopers with the resources to live in a manner grander than that of his parents. The mix of styles and periods can be seen as the starting point for Terence's contagiously successful approach to interior decorating. He remembered seeing the paintings in a very different way when they were hung on the walls of their house in Liphook, stripped of their frames. His parents had sold the frames to pay for his school fees. Terence thought that they looked much better when the gilt had gone.

It was considered normal in family life at the time for middle-class parents to maintain a certain distance from their children. Terence's nanny, Jenny Envis, played an important role in bringing him up. He was sent to his first boarding school aged just six, where he met Alexander Plunket Greene, the future husband of Mary Quant. When the air raids began after the outbreak of war, the Conran family moved out of London again, renting Old Shepherd's Farm, a house on the edge of Liphook in Hampshire, an hour from the capital. When peace came, they commissioned an architect to build a modern house for them near the town's golf club.

Terence transferred from Boxgrove, his first boarding school, to become a day boy at Highfield, a prep school two fields away from their house.

Highfield was a conventional enough English prep school, with a clergyman for its headmaster. It was geared up for preparing its pupils, most of whom were boarders, to take the Common Entrance Exam for admission to Eton, Winchester or Marlborough. Refusing to conform to stereotypes for creative schoolboys, Terence seems to have been happy at Highfield. He played cricket and rugby, and learned carpentry and metalwork. In a school photograph taken in the summer of 1942, Terence stands out from the rest of his class of eleven-year-olds wearing suits and ties only because of his double-breasted jacket.

There were nights when German bombers, on their way to attack Portsmouth's naval base, forced the family to take cover under the kitchen table. The neighbouring farm was set ablaze after one air raid. Conran and Co.'s warehouse in Stepney was hit in another raid. It took days to put the fires out, and Terence remembered seeing the ruins with the 'molten residue of its contents congealed like toffee on the pavement'.[2] This was a setback from which his father's business did not recover. Rupert Conran then became a salesman for Docker Brothers, a large paint firm based in Birmingham. His many contacts with architects who specified Docker products for their buildings would be useful to Terence in the future. But for Terence, the experience of seeing his father accept his new position as an employee rather than an owner seems to have stimulated his determination to make a success of himself. Terence believed that his father did not have the same entrepreneurial spirit that drove both his children.

AN EDUCATION IN THE ARTS AND CRAFTS

After the destruction of Rupert Conran's gum-importing business during the war, he used his expertise as a salesman for Docker Brothers, supplying architects with the paints that they needed for major building projects

There was rationing for almost everything, from food to clothing and furniture, but the war impacted the Conrans less than many other families. Terence's father was not called up for military service, and the two children stayed with their parents, rather than being evacuated to live with strangers.

In an early sign of Terence's enterprising instincts, he used his skills to make things that he could sell, from dolls' house furniture to ashtrays. He used to make impressively detailed model ships and trains. He swapped one of them with Charles Lane, the owner of the Royal Anchor in Liphook, who had an extensive model railway in the pub garden on a scale large enough to carry passengers, in exchange for a three-and-a-half-inch Myford metal-turning lathe. This enabled Terence to take on ever more elaborate engineering projects. But acquiring that lathe led to an accident with far-reaching consequences when he was thirteen years old. While he was working to shape a piece of metal, a fragment spun off from the lathe and stuck in one of his eyes.

He wasn't completely blinded in the affected eye, he could make out light and dark, and there was no visible sign of the damage. He always shrugged off this potentially traumatic episode, adapting quickly, and learning to play cricket left-handed. Despite the accident, he remained an enthusiastic maker. It was a fascination that contributed to the decision of his parents to send him to Bryanston, a school that placed great emphasis on practical and creative skills, rather than one of the more traditional public schools for which Highfield prepared most of its boys.

Terence started at Bryanston at the beginning of 1945, just five months before the end of the Second World War. He missed his first term because of a burst appendix that gave him a life-threatening case of peritonitis. He spent six months being nursed back to recovery. Terence could remember seeing his parents in tears as they took in just how serious their eldest child's condition was.

Clem Attlee's Labour Government came to power during Terence's first summer at Bryanston, and it embarked on the social and economic transformation of Britain. It nationalised the steel industry, coalmines and railways, established the National Health Service, and granted independence to India, the largest of Britain's colonial possessions. But everyday life remained bleak. Despite the birth of the welfare state, bread went on ration for the first time in 1946, and fuel shortages meant that the school building was heated only intermittently. It was a period when the entire country was obliged to limit the amount of hot water used in baths to no more than a few inches a week.

Bryanston was, and still is, housed in a colossal country house, designed by the gifted Victorian architect Norman Shaw – who was also responsible for the original Scotland Yard building for the Metropolitan Police; Cragside, a prodigious mansion in Northumberland; and laying out Bedford Park, the garden suburb in West London, among much else. The magnificence of Bryanston's building runs somewhat counter to the moderately progressive lines along which the school is run. Shaw built Bryanston between 1889 and 1894 for the second Viscount Portman. Flush with an avalanche of cash from the ground rents paid by the Portman Estate in London, the viscount demolished an existing classical house and spent

At Bryanston, Terence made drawings and woodcuts that were used in the school magazine

AN EDUCATION IN THE ARTS AND CRAFTS

the equivalent of £20 million on building a much more ostentatious replacement. Bryanston was not quite the last of England's great Victorian country houses, but it was close.

Bryanston sits amid 450 acres, near the old market town of Blandford Forum. Its red-brick facades, monumental windows edged in stone and the cavernous grandeur of its interiors give it the look of a French chateau from the Loire Valley transplanted to the lush Dorset countryside. A central block stands on the edge of a series of terraced formal gardens, under steep mansard roofs, with lower wings stepping back on either side. Less than thirty years after the house was completed, the Portman family was forced to sell it to pay death duties, at a price far below what it had cost to build. In 1928 Bryanston became a boarding school for boys from the age of thirteen, set up by an Australian schoolmaster called Jeffrey Graham Jeffreys.

Jeffreys based the school on an educational philosophy formulated in America known as the Dalton system, which involves tailoring a programme to individual pupils. Followers of the system believe that it gives students a sense of personal responsibility for their education. As if they were a university student, each child is allocated a personal tutor, who reviews their progress, and directs them towards the classes and programmes best suited to them. Jeffreys was followed by Thorold Coade, who stayed as headmaster for almost thirty years.

Bryanston did not go as far as co-educational Dartington Hall, which had been started two years earlier, and ruled out all forms of punishment as well as rejecting compulsory games and religious observance. Coade did not believe in the use of corporal punishment, nor in the fagging system, but there were rules and there were prefects. In Terence's time, it was a single-sex school. Boys who misbehaved were sent on a run from the main door of the school to the lodge gates at the end of the drive, with multiple lengths prescribed for the more serious offenders, among which Terence suggested that he was numbered. Early on, Coade raised the funds to be able to offer a substantial number of free places to local children whose families could not afford the fees. There was a sister school for girls at nearby Cranborne Chase, whose pupils took part in some of Bryanston's activities. The school regime was a compromise between the radical and the familiar that helped Bryanston attract well-to-do parents looking for an alternative to traditional public schools for their sons.

It quickly earned a reputation for nurturing creative talent. Lucian Freud went there after spending a year at Dartington Hall. Howard Hodgkin studied in the art room at Bryanston alongside Terence, after trying Eton. Richard Burton, who established the distinguished architectural practice of Ahrends, Burton and Koralek, and designed Habitat's buildings in Wallingford for Terence, was also a pupil. So was Adrian Heath – who went on to become a painter at the Slade art school, which was at that time still in Oxford to where it had been evacuated at the start of the war – alongside Paolozzi, Richard Hamilton and Nigel Henderson.

Coade was mocked for running a school where the boys could do what they liked. His reply was that 'they like what they do'. He introduced 'pioneering' as an alternative to the Combined Cadet Force military training offered at more traditional public schools. Pupils took part in construction projects and estate management around the Bryanston grounds. Among other things, Terence helped to build an open-air Greek theatre, a boathouse and an observatory. 'I learnt how to lay a brick, and wipe a plumbing joint,' he once said.[3]

Bryanston's art department was exceptional, staffed by a succession of significant artists. Willi Soukop, a sculptor from Vienna who had been at Dartington, set up the sculpture course during the war. The abstract painter Roger Hilton, who had studied at the Slade and subsequently in Paris, was another of Terence's teachers. The head of the art department for Terence's years at the school was Charles Handley-Read, who had been part of the first intake of Bryanston pupils. Handley-Read went back to Bryanston after taking an architecture degree at Cambridge. By the time Terence started, Handley-Read, a conscientious objector, had only recently returned from serving at the epileptic colony at Lingfield where he had spent most of the war as an alternative to military service. He was a passionate collector of the decorative art of the high-Victorian architect William Burges. His scholarship played a significant part in the taste revolution that saw the rediscovery of Burges in the 1970s. He introduced Howard Hodgkin to the work of Wyndham Lewis. He was, however, a fragile personality who eventually committed suicide in 1971 at the age of fifty-five.

But the teacher who had the most direct impact on Terence was Don Potter, a charismatic figure and a considerable artist. Potter had worked with Eric Gill for six years before Bryanston. He stayed at the school for more than forty years, living long enough to see the opening of a new studio for the art department named after him, and reaching the age of 102.

Fiona MacCarthy describes Potter climbing scaffolding to be interviewed for an apprenticeship by Gill, who was dressed in a cassock while working on his sculpture of Ariel high up on the facade of the new BBC building on Portland Place. Potter became Gill's principal assistant, executing a series of substantial commissions under his direction. Potter moved to live at Pigotts, Gill's home and workshop in the Chilterns, staying almost until the time of his deeply flawed mentor's death in 1940. MacCarthy's biography of Gill is sympathetic but includes a shocking account of Gill's abuse of his family. Potter combined the teaching of

AN EDUCATION IN THE ARTS AND CRAFTS

Bryanston School in Dorset, designed by Norman Shaw, was originally built as a grand country house. It became a boy's school in the 1920s

Art and craft were particular strengths of Bryanston's curriculum. Lucian Freud and Howard Hodgkin both studied at the school, and a number of distinguished artists taught there

Don Potter, a charismatic teacher and a former assistant to Eric Gill, was an accomplished sculptor himself. This larger-than-life-sized representation of Baden-Powell carved in granite stands outside the Scout movement's headquarters in London

sculpture, metalwork and pottery with an active career as a sculptor in his own right, mainly working on representational art designed for architectural settings. His best-known work is the ten-foot figure of Baden-Powell carved in granite at the headquarters of the Boy Scout movement in South Kensington.

With no previous experience of working with clay, Potter asked Amy Krauss, a former student of Bernard Leach in St Ives, to teach him the basics at her pottery close by in Corfe Castle. As he mastered the technique, he explored the formal qualities of pottery with Michael Cardew, another of Leach's former apprentices. Potter took his pupils, Terence among them, to see Katherine Pleydell-Bouverie at work in her studio at Coleshill. He was an enthusiastic believer in the use of local materials. He dug his own clay, and he made his own glazes and encouraged his pupils to do the same.

Don Potter taught Terence how to build a kiln as well as the basics of ceramics, and most importantly showed him the pleasures of making an object

For Potter's 100th birthday, Terence presented his former teacher with a collection of a dozen pieces of progressive contemporary ceramics. He was aware that they might not be to Potter's taste, but the expectation was that they would one day be left to Bryanston. In her obituary for Potter, Fiona MacCarthy described his studio as follows: 'the pottery was in a cellar, down a dark, dusty, spiral stone staircase, where he could be found, like an alchemist, working in the bowels of the building with wheels turning, clay flying and kilns roaring'.[4] He built a wood-fired kiln for earthenware himself, and there are many memories among ex-pupils of staying up for all-night firings, drinking illicit beer and cider while Potter reminisced and quoted William Blake. Terence spoke of the way in which Potter had given

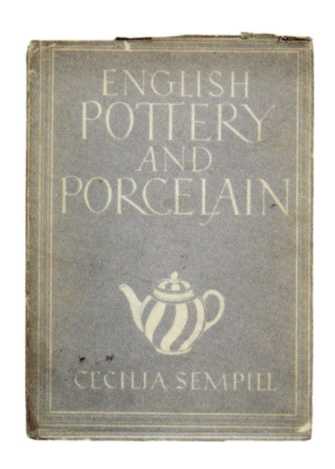

Terence kept his textbooks from the 1940s. Pottery was a special pleasure for him, but he also had books on engineering and workshop practice

him the chance to experience 'the glow you can get from seeing an idea turn into a three-dimensional, beautiful object'.[5]

Potter's pupils helped him to build a kiln at the school, and Terence used what he had learned from the experience to make one of his own at home. He made a pottery wheel at school too, recycling a scrapped camshaft. He brought it home to join his lathe in the garden shed that became his first studio. Screen-printing equipment would follow later. During at least one school holiday, Terence got a job at the Wrecclesham commercial pottery within cycling distance of Liphook. He made clay flowerpots, digging up the clay, pugging it, turning it on a manual wheel and then firing it – an experience that would one day be reflected in the addition to the Habitat catalogue of the chicken brick, made in the same way. 'Habitat's own chicken brick revives a centuries-old cooking tradition, sealing the flavour of the meat, rather than allowing it to go up the chimney', suggested the 1971 catalogue. It also showed the fish brick, and the parsley pot: 'grow your own indoors. All hand thrown, on traditional potter's wheels by craftsmen who become rarer year by year.' Terence acquired Cecilia Sempill's book *English Pottery and Porcelain*, as well as William Ruscoe's *A Manual for the Potter*, and kept them all his life.

The time he spent in what had been the below-stairs world of the servants' quarters at Bryanston made a lasting impression on Terence. He lived in a dormitory in Connaught House, and in his last year he got a study of his own. But he often spoke of preferring the plain, simple working kitchens of stately houses to the grander elaboration of the fine rooms. It was as much a reflection of Terence's instinctive suspicion of privilege as an aesthetic argument.

Terence certainly enjoyed Bryanston: he sent three of his four sons there, and later his stepdaughter Hattie, whom he brought up with his fourth wife Vicki. During his lifetime, he would reconnect with the boys he knew at school, and even some of his teachers. Bryanston remained important to him. He became a governor and helped to fund the building of the school's arts centre, though he insisted on an architect of his choice to design it.

There was little tradition of university education in either of his parents' families. Terence claimed to have briefly considered the idea of an apprenticeship to a gunmaker when he was given a shotgun as a teenager by a relative. It was not, he would say, because he was interested in shooting for its own sake, but rather that he was fascinated by the mix of engineering skill and craftsmanship that went into the making of a British sporting gun. He suggested that he abandoned the idea when he understood quite how long the apprenticeship would take.

The pleasure he had taken in pottery and working in metal opened his mind to the possibility of going to art school. Priscilla Conran, who went to Cranborne Chase before she studied photography at art school in Surrey, would follow the same route as her brother. Britain's art schools had not yet been turned into universities, and were far smaller institutions than they have since become. Admission was based much more on the quality of the applicant's portfolio and a personal interview than on school examinations.

Charles Handley-Read encouraged Terence to think about taking the textile design course at the Central School. Unlike studio pottery, which genuinely fascinated Terence, textile design, which was new to him, seemed to offer a more promising direction for a career. The Central School's printed textiles course had a reputation for producing graduates with marketable skills. Potter would also have been an influence on his decision to try for the Central School, since Eric Gill had studied calligraphy there, taught by Edward Johnston, who designed the typeface still used today by the London Underground.

The Central School of Arts and Crafts, as it was known when this building first opened in 1908, was designed by its first director, William Lethaby. Its Portland stone and granite facades were as progressive as anything Edwardian Britain had built

AN EDUCATION IN THE ARTS AND CRAFTS

Textile design at the Central School was taught by Dora Batty. She was a respected teacher and a gifted designer, working for, among many other clients, London Transport

Terence was interviewed for a place on the course by Dora Batty, a distinguished illustrator and graphic designer with posters for London Transport, ceramics for the Poole Pottery and graphics for Mac Fisheries to her credit. Batty was a long-serving teacher at the Central School, who became the head of the textile school in 1950. She was impressed enough by Terence's portfolio to offer him one of the dozen places on the course, for which there was a lot of demand; the whole department never had more than forty students. Terence's damaged eye allowed him to avoid national service and the limbo of spending eighteen months in uniform, and so he arrived in London in the autumn of 1948 as a student. At first he commuted from Liphook, taking an early train to Waterloo to get to the school in Holborn in time for the start of classes, which the highly organised Dora Batty insisted should start on time and fill the whole day. If these were not in the studio or in the lecture theatre, they were at the Victoria and Albert Museum (V&A), where Terence would sketch antique textiles from its collection. Terence had vivid memories of his time in the museum, examining antique Byzantine weaving and seventeenth-century Indian miniatures. To judge by the illustrations in Terence's first book, *Printed Textile Design*, published in 1957, he also spent time looking at eighteenth-century Persian silk, German resist-dyed linen from the late seventeenth century and early Chinese porcelain, as well as the British Museum's collection of adinkra funeral cloths and Anglo-Saxon carvings. At least some of these inspirations were the suggestions of Shirley Pearce, his second wife, who was studying painting at Chelsea College of Art when she met him and went on to take a weaving course at the Central School.

There would also be an evening class on most days of the week, timed to accommodate the many part-timers who combined work with study, after which Terence caught the train back to Hampshire and his parents. After a term of this, Terence's mother found him a room in a house belonging to an actor in Paultons Square in Chelsea. Using the first clothing ration coupons issued to him in his own right, he bought himself a viridian drape jacket, a yellow shirt and beige drainpipe trousers from Cecil Gee, and emerged looking like a Teddy Boy. The shop on Shaftesbury Avenue was the forerunner of the Carnaby Street phenomenon. It was started by Sasha Goldstein, an East End tailor born in Lithuania, who arrived in London as a ten-year-old and moved his business from Commercial Road to the West End after the war in search of more affluent customers.

Going to the Central School, which relied on teaching practical skills in its workshops, was a natural step for any student who had thrived in the art rooms at Bryanston. It was established in 1896 by London County Council under the leadership of William Lethaby, an architect who had been Norman Shaw's chief assistant

AN EDUCATION IN THE ARTS AND CRAFTS

Lethaby based the Central School's teaching methods on the ideas of William Morris. Students learned by making in the school's workshops, an approach that inspired Walter Gropius' plans for the Bauhaus

for ten years before leaving in 1889 just prior to the commission for Bryanston. He had been a prime mover in establishing the Art Workers' Guild in 1884, and was a committed socialist, a friend of William Morris and acquainted with Ruskin. He asked May Morris, the daughter of William Morris and Jane Burden, and an employee of Morris and Co., to run the embroidery department.

Lethaby was responsible for the design of the Central School's gaunt, high-ceilinged building in Holborn on Southampton Row, where it moved to in 1908. His design served as an architectural manifesto for the school, just as Walter Gropius's building in Dessau had encapsulated the Bauhaus in 1925. Lethaby's building, however, empty since 2011 when the school moved to King's Cross, looks like a historical curiosity rather than a model for others to follow. It is representative neither of familiar Arts and Crafts comfort, nor of the austere modernity that Adolf Loos was already building in Vienna, but a disconcerting mix of both, as if caught incomplete in the middle of a shape-shifting stylistic transition. The Central School has turned out to be more durable than the Bauhaus, both as an institution, and in the physical sense. But in photographs the Central School's soot-streaked massive granite and Portland stone walls are in stark contrast to the dazzling white, if fragile, cement render of Gropius's Bauhaus.

It has been claimed that without the Central School, there would have been no Bauhaus. Walter Gropius certainly leaned heavily on the Arts and Crafts tradition in his prospectus establishing the Bauhaus in 1919. Like the Central School, the Bauhaus was based on teaching through workshops. Since its foundation the Central School had embodied a paradox: modernity was a product of the Machine Age, and yet its teaching methods were based on handicrafts. It was the same tension that could be seen in Nikolaus Pevsner's attempts to claim William Morris as the forefather of the Modern movement, despite Morris's visceral rejection of the machine. In fact, the Bauhaus itself had been similarly conflicted. Walter Gropius had used the terminology of the Art Workers' Guild, of masters and apprentices, even as the school became closely associated with the aesthetics of the Machine Age.

In Terence's day, the influence was in the opposite direction, with new ideas flowing from mainland Europe to Britain. As he learned more about the history of design, he became increasingly taken with the Bauhaus and the work of its teachers. William Johnstone, an accomplished Scottish painter trained in Paris, who was the principal after the war, brought an international perspective to the school. He employed refugees including the textile designer Hans Tisdall, the Bauhaus graduate Naum Slutzky, and Anton Ehrenzweig, an artist and intellectual who arrived in Britain in 1938 from Vienna after the Anschluss, in which Austria was annexed by Nazi Germany.

Johnstone transformed the Central School's approach to the teaching of industrial design, a course that until 1948 had been run by a silversmith. In Terence's time, the prospectus described industrial design as 'a basic course in the theory of design and the technology of machine processes'. He released the school from the medievalism that coloured William Morris's version of the idea of the arts and crafts, and his prejudice against industrialisation, by injecting contemporary culture into the courses. It took time for this modernisation to be formally recognised. It was only in 1966 that the school, now Central Saint Martins, a part of the University of the Arts, London, was renamed the Central School of Art and Design. Snipping

Edward Johnston, the typographer who had taught Eric Gill calligraphy at the Central School, and who was commissioned by Frank Pick to design the typeface that is still in use on the London Underground

AN EDUCATION IN THE ARTS AND CRAFTS

The Central School's textile studio in the 1940s, where Anton Ehrenzweig and Eduardo Paolozzi taught

A student textile print by Terence from 1947 or 1948

the final 's' from 'arts' to make it 'art' reflected a move away from the applied and decorative arts towards the higher status of simply art. 'Design', a word with a long history rooted in drawing, reflects a very different ideology from the utopianism of the 'craft' revival. It sounded self-consciously modern. Design, Terence remembered, was a word that had not yet become current when he was a student. It was more often described as 'commercial art', a qualification intended to distinguish it from pure art and a reflection of its relative lack of status as an academic subject.

Ehrenzweig began a fabric printing class at the Central School in 1949 and ran the school's dye room. He involved Terence in silkscreen-printing work for Zika Ascher, who came from a Czech mill-owning family and had been a champion skier before the war. Ascher and his wife fled to London as refugees and subsequently started their textile business in 1944. After the war, Ascher was able to sell his fabrics to French fashion houses for their couture collections. He began an artist's squares project, producing silk scarves in limited editions. He persuaded Henry Moore, Pablo Picasso, André Derain and Alexander Calder to take part. In 1947 Ascher went to see the invalid Henri Matisse in his Boulevard Montparnasse apartment in Paris; two distinct projects emerged from this visit. There was a silk twill square, in two different versions designated simply as *Echape A* and *Echape B*, each in editions of 275, like the other artist's squares produced by Ascher. More ambitious was *Oceanie, le Ciel*, an edition of thirty wall hangings on cambric almost four metres wide, designed using paper cuts that Matisse instructed his assistant to position on the walls of his studio according to his exact directions in memory of a past journey to the Pacific. This was printed in Northern Ireland by Zdenek Sochor, an émigré from Czechoslovakia who started an advanced textile printing factory in Belfast. In London Ascher worked with a number of skilled printers. According to Terence, Ascher contracted Ehrenzweig to take on the printing of Matisse's designs for the smaller scarves. Ehrenzweig in turn paid Terence and some of his other students to help him with the work in his tiny studio in Shepherd Market. Terence remembered being impressed that Ascher had been able to source silk and cambric for the project with rationing still in force, and shortages of materials of all kinds. A maquette was prepared by Matisse and sent to London where Ehrenzweig, with the assistance of some of his students, used what were described to Matisse as photographic techniques to allay his concerns that his work was going to be interpreted rather than reproduced. They prepared the screens that were then used to print the fabric, which was sent back to Paris for Matisse to sign each piece individually. Matisse followed every step of the process in demanding detail, asking for samples of the fabric, and insisting that his intentions were followed faithfully.

AN EDUCATION IN THE ARTS AND CRAFTS

Nigel Henderson, a self-portrait

Henderson's photograph of Eduardo Paolozzi

Under Ehrenzweig's direction, Terence helped to make silkscreens using large sheets of a light-sensitive acetate known as Kodatrace. He traced the images of Matisse's paper cuts using a brush and opaque paint. Almost sixty years later he could recall the process step by step. He remembered preparing the screens by coating them with a gelatine and iodine paste. The Kodatrace sheet, which faithfully reproduced Matisse's design, was placed on the stretched silk and exposed to light for up to six hours. The painted areas of the sheet protected the paste on the silkscreen beneath from setting. It was then washed away, leaving a screen that looked like a negative of Matisse's original. The next step was to mix the dyes with gum tragacanth, and then to use a big rubber squeegee to press the colour through the parts of the screen that had been left clear, on to the fabric below.

Aside from hiring accomplished refugees, Johnstone's other innovation for the Central School was to appoint younger artists to the technical departments, including William Turnbull, Richard Hamilton and Henderson, a group who already knew each other from their time at the Slade. He wrote to Paolozzi, who was living in Paris at the time, to offer him a teaching job too. Paolozzi said that he took his time replying, and later claimed to have been punished for it by being allocated to the textile department rather than to the sculpture course. But he was being supported financially by Freda Elliot, the textile designer he married in 1951 and, although she worked front of house at the Institute of Contemporary Arts (ICA), they needed the money. Paolozzi was also attracted by the chance of using the Central School's workshops, foundry and kilns, and so he started work during Terence's second

TERENCE CONRAN   MAKING MODERN BRITAIN

AN EDUCATION IN THE ARTS AND CRAFTS

Three works of sculpture by Eduardo Paolozzi. One of them, *Suwasa*, was originally placed at the Economist Plaza in London by Alison and Peter Smithson. Two more, *Trishula* and *Kalasan*, were commissioned by Terence. They were brought together at the Habitat warehouse in Wallingford, which was designed by Ahrends, Burton and Koralek. Fabricated from aluminium, using industrial welding and extruding techniques, they were intended to form a robust playground for the children of Habitat's customers

year. Ida Kar, a photographer who specialised in recording the artists of the period, portrayed Paolozzi. Kar had come to London from Egypt with her husband Victor Musgrave, who established Gallery One in Soho. Musgrave employed John Kasmin and helped him to start on his own career as an independent gallerist.

Paolozzi, born to Italian parents in Leith in 1924, had studied sculpture at the Slade immediately after the war. The Mayor Gallery, to which he was introduced by Henderson's well-connected mother Wyn – who had once worked for and then quarrelled with Nancy Cunard, and then ran Peggy Guggenheim's gallery in London – gave him a one man show of his drawings in 1947. Sales of that work financed his stay in Paris, where he rented a cheap room on the Île Saint-Louis. He enrolled at the École des Beaux-Arts, but said he never went there and took to inviting himself to the studios of artists including Constantin Brancusi, Georges Braque and Fernand Léger. He established a closer relationship with Alberto Giacometti, and produced a series of experimental sculptures under his influence.

Once Paolozzi started at the Central School, he and Terence became close, though stick-thin Terence and barrel-chested Paolozzi were an unlikely couple. Terence had lived out the war in Hampshire. Paolozzi, who was seven years older, had faced a much harsher life. As a teenager he spent his summers at Fascist youth summer camps in Italy. When Italy declared war on Britain in June 1940, he was locked up in a cell as an enemy alien. He was in Saughton, a bleak prison on the outskirts of Edinburgh, for three months. His father and his uncle drowned in the same year, when the ship taking them to Canada as internees was torpedoed by the Germans.

The relationship with Paolozzi was to be enormously important for Terence – first as a student, then as an assistant, later as a friend and patron. Hamilton described Terence as 'following him everywhere'. Terence still wore his grey school suit when

Eduardo Paolozzi's *Head of Invention* was originally placed outside the Design Museum at Shad Thames in 1989, and moved to its new home in Kensington in 2016

Thomas Heatherwick's Gazebo at Barton Court

they first met, while Paolozzi, intellectually sophisticated though he was, dressed in uncompromising workman's denim. Twenty-five years later, when Richard Burton designed Habitat's Wallingford building in 1973, Terence asked Paolozzi to make a playground for the site. Paolozzi produced two new works: *Trishula* and *Kalasan*. He combined them with *Suwasa*, a piece that he had originally made a decade earlier for the Economist Plaza, designed by his friends Alison and Peter Smithson. All three pieces were made from aluminium, using industrial techniques in a workshop in Ipswich, and boldly geometrical in their form. Standing together as a group, they were designed to invite adventurous children to climb all over them.

Terence celebrated the opening of the first Design Museum building in 1989 by commissioning another work from Paolozzi, a large bronze piece *Head of Invention*, that was placed on the riverfront at Shad Thames, where it also became a climbing frame. It was later moved to the museum's new home in Kensington. In 1957 Terence wrote that Paolozzi is 'one of the few who have reason to be convinced of their own genius; he is not only a textile designer, but one of the most powerful sculptors of this age'.[6] Long afterwards, Terence was equally enthusiastic in his praise for the creativity of Thomas Heatherwick. Upon seeing Heatherwick's degree show piece, Gazebo, Terence invited him to Barton Court to discuss building it there. He subsequently bought it and had it installed in the garden.

When Terence first met him, Paolozzi was working with a wide range of artistic languages simultaneously. He was making collages with lurid images taken from American magazines, juxtaposing film stars with labels from canned tuna and tinned fruit. But he was also making formal sculpture influenced by Alberto Giacometti, working in clay and bronze, and looking at non-Western art. It was a world away from Don Potter's somewhat glum representational work.

In an attempt to break the ice with his students, Paolozzi spent his sweet ration on a block of toffee. He used a hammer to smash it to make enough fragments to distribute to every one of them. Terence remembered the impact that Paolozzi ('handsome in an unexpected way') had on his overwhelmingly female class – 'thirty, or sometimes thirty-two, virgins from Surbiton', as Terence always put it.

Most students quickly began to produce work that looked much like that of their teacher, which may explain why Paolozzi complained to Terence:

The trouble with most students I find is that they are too self-conscious. They work the design up until all the magic is lost: they try too hard to apply what they have learned, instead of accepting the fact that they have absorbed it; they are inclined to regard their teachers with awe ... il maestro, you know ... and don't think, or criticise for themselves. As regards colour, students don't look closely enough at primitive work, and look too closely at what sells; this subconsciously influences them. Perhaps not so subconsciously.[7]

Paolozzi taught Terence about pattern-making and collage. As their relationship deepened, he also showed him how to slice an onion properly, and how to cook risotto using ingredients from Italy such as olive oil and squid ink. This was at a time when, in most of Britain, olive oil was only to be found on sale in miniature bottles in chemists as a medicinal product; even buying a clove of garlic meant a trip to a Soho specialist.

When Paolozzi discovered that Terence knew how to weld and print, he started to make use of his skills as a studio assistant. Henderson, who was living in the East End at the time, found a workshop space for them in Bunsen Street close to his house. Terence worked there with Paolozzi, making his sculptures, manipulating steel rods, welding pieces together. He also used the space to make his own projects as he started to find his first commissions.

'I got my oxyacetylene welding kit set up there, and Eduardo brought tons of stuff in,' Terence remembered. 'I started to weld armatures, that he covered with plaster, which then went off to be cast in bronze at the foundry.' It was here that Terence started to make furniture, initially for his own use. It began as a shared activity with Paolozzi. 'I welded a structure that he would put a tiled top on,'

AN EDUCATION IN THE ARTS AND CRAFTS

Eduardo Paolozzi working on a plaster sculpture, 1950

Nigel Henderson, *Man in Bunsen Street, Bethnal Green*, where Paolozzi's workshop was based, 1950

Table at the ICA, Dover Street, designed by Paolozzi and Terence, 1950

Eduardo Paolozzi, the Smithsons and Nigel Henderson, *Parallel of Life and Art*, exhibition at the ICA, 1953

Richard Hamilton, *Growth and Form*, exhibition at the ICA, 1951

Terence remembered.[8] At the same time, he was helping Paolozzi with his work. He recalled working on one particular table sculpture in 1949 titled *Growth*. It was a cast bronze version of a work Paolozzi had made in Paris in plaster.

A little later, when Terence began to make commercial furniture to order, he would use Paolozzi's textiles, as he did for the chairs he made in 1950 for the Ridgeway Hotel in Lusaka that he designed while working for the architect Dennis Lennon.

Henderson took an apparently snatched photograph, now in the collection of the Tate, showing the street in which Paolozzi's workshop once stood. It captured the essential bleakness of the East End in 1948, where the only colour seemed to come from purple weeds sprouting over an archipelago of bombed sites. Art did not form part of the world of most Britons of Terence's background. He grew up in a period in which the country was conventionally described as being more literary in its cultural tastes than visual. But that was not the case for Terence. The artists that surrounded him at school and at the Central School, the world to which Paolozzi introduced him, shaped his life, and gave him an eclectic range of enthusiasms and connections.

There were moments when Terence seemed on the brink of moving from being a spectator to becoming a part of that community of artists. He found himself involved with the ICA, which began life as a conversation between Roland Penrose and Herbert Read at Penrose's house in Hampstead in 1946. Among its early guiding influences was the architect Jane Drew and Marcus Brumwell – who, with Read, was a co-founder of the Design Research Unit, Britain's first professional design consultancy.

The ICA briefly attempted to become London's version of New York's Museum of Modern Art, before setting up in an Edwardian townhouse at 17 Dover Street that opened in 1950 as an institute, rather than a museum. Its early visitors included Le Corbusier, whose paintings, tapestries and sculpture were exhibited there in 1953. It is where the pre-war modernists associated with Paris and Surrealism arranged a largely peaceful handover of the reins of the avant-garde to a post-war generation that saw itself as tougher-minded than its predecessors.

Drew was close to Paolozzi, and it's possible that connection helped Terence get his first job from Dennis Lennon, a former employee of Max Fry and Drew, when he went looking for a bright assistant. In her interviews for the British Library's oral history project, Drew talked about travelling with Paolozzi to Italy. Paolozzi called Drew a patron. She commissioned him to make a fountain sculpture at the Festival of Britain that Conran helped with, and to design a mural for her own office. She was also the architect for the conversion of a house on Dover Street that was the first home of the ICA, where she asked Paolozzi, assisted by Terence, to design and build the bar.

Terence followed Paolozzi as far as the outer edge of a circle of artists, writers and architects that would become known as the Independent Group, an informal cluster of people associated with the ICA who gathered to talk and socialise, but also to exhibit together.

They met initially at the home of Reyner Banham, who was still completing a doctorate at the Courtauld Institute when he joined the staff of the *Architectural Review*, and then in the members' room at Dover Street, which Paolozzi had decorated with the help of Terence. There is a photograph taken in 1950 which shows the entrance lobby with a table credited by the ICA as having been designed by both Terence and Paolozzi. It has a rough-cast thick concrete slab as a top, which is probably Paolozzi's contribution. The concrete is supported on splayed steel-rod legs. Beneath the concrete top, an open frame has been welded to the legs, criss-crossed by ropework to create a basket-like shelf. Terence used the same rope technique for a chair that he sold to the architect Colin St John Wilson for his own use, and, through a complicated chain of coincidences, to Picasso. This involved a designer called Toby Jellinek who had worked for Terence after leaving Summerhill, the progressive school established by AS Neill. Jellinek had moved to France with his nineteen-year-old girlfriend, Sylvette David, in 1954. They took a room in the small town of Vallauris, near Antibes, where Picasso had a studio. Picasso met them at an exhibition and, after Jellinek had given him a version of one the chairs that he had been making for Terence, Picasso asked the strikingly beautiful Sylvette to model for him. More than forty works emerged from these sessions, showing the young Sylvette as the striking girl with the ponytail.

The Independent Group staged a series of presentations at the ICA, including *Bunk,* Paolozzi's lecture without words in 1952 that took the form of projecting apparently random images from his collection of artefacts of popular culture. This is often described as the birth of Pop art, with the images becoming the subject of a sequence of screen prints.

Richard Hamilton's ground-breaking exhibitions at the ICA mixed photography, collage and space-making, the first of which, *Growth and Form*, was held in the summer of 1951. There was an exhibition on town planning in London, and for just two weeks in the spring of 1952 *Tomorrow's Furniture*, which was organised by Ian McCallum and JM Richards. The *Architectural Review*'s coverage of this in August was surprisingly cold, given that two of its editors had put it on. 'Some sixty designers were invited to submit designs for contemporary furniture in the prototype stage. This probably accounted for the notable absence of several

AN EDUCATION IN THE ARTS AND CRAFTS

Nigel Henderson's self-portrait with Alison and Peter Smithson and Eduardo Paolozzi, Limerston Street, taken for the *This is Tomorrow* exhibition at the Whitechapel Gallery

outstanding newcomers such as Terence Conran and Bernard Schottlander.'⁹ In 1953, Henderson, Paolozzi and the Smithsons staged *Parallel of Life and Art*, and Terence helped Paolozzi with realising the striking installation. With its extensive use of angled panels suspended from the ceiling, and enlarged found images, it reflected the spatial character of the restaurants that Terence was designing at the time.

Adrian Heath's studio at the top of a tall, thin Georgian house at 22 Fitzroy Street has long since been demolished. But over three weekends from 1952 to 1953, sandwiched between the cash-in-hand, second-hand car dealers south of Warren Street, and the restaurants of Charlotte Street, staffed by Austrian refugees, closer to Oxford Street, it was a place for self-organised gatherings of artists and designers of a slightly more ecumenical nature than the Independent Group allowed. At the time, this was the closest London got to the Left Bank in Paris, a temporary bohemia peopled by hard-drinking veterans of the war now in London to complete their education as mature students, and the artists and architects who taught them.

Heath was a pioneer of British abstract painting, who had been at Bryanston in 1930. His time at the Slade was interrupted by the war, much of which he spent in a German prison camp after the Lancaster bomber in which he had been a tail gunner was shot down. He went back to the Slade in 1945, where he encountered Paolozzi, Henderson and Hamilton. Heath presided over a number of informal, short-lived exhibitions in his studio that were a chance for people to show a variety of work. Terence took part in the last of them, which ran over the first four days of May. He dropped off a low table and a couple of chairs in his van, and they went on to show alongside a Paolozzi collage and one of Henderson's photographic murals.

In all there were sixteen exhibitors, including Ben Nicholson, Victor Pasmore and Roger Hilton, another former prisoner of war, who had spent almost three years as a German prisoner after being captured during the Dieppe commando raid. He had moved from teaching at Bryanston to the Central School. There was also William Scott and the textile designer Vera Spencer, who had studied textile design at the Central School a year ahead of Terence. Spencer, who was married to Herbert Spencer, editor of *Typographica*, was singled out for praise in Toni del Renzio's report in *Art News and Review*, and Terence would later show her work in his own basement showroom in the Piccadilly Arcade. Del Renzio, a Russian-born Surrealist artist, designer and critic, was less complimentary about Terence, whose contribution he described as being 'in the Paolozzi manner, a smooth version of a Chiavari chair'.¹⁰ In total, 150 people signed the visitors' book. The design of the invitation card has been attributed to Herbert Spencer, but Anthony Froshaug, the

AN EDUCATION IN THE ARTS AND CRAFTS

Kasmin commissioned Richard Burton of Ahrends, Burton and Koralek to design his first gallery on New Bond Street. It had the space to show large-scale contemporary art that ranged from David Hockney to Anthony Caro, as well as American artists such as Frank Stella and Kenneth Noland

brilliant graphic designer who taught at the Central School and at the Hochschule Ulm, is another possibility.

It was in this same Fitzroy Street studio that the first conversations about staging the *This is Tomorrow* exhibition took place. It would be organised by Theo Crosby and for once held at the Whitechapel Gallery rather than the ICA.

Henderson used a delayed exposure to take the defining image of the Independent Group – missing Hamilton – for the exhibition catalogue in 1956. They are arranged seated on a range of significant pieces of furniture drawn up in the middle of the street. Rendered in bleak black and white, with a sparse scattering of elderly motor cars, at first sight it looks like the East End. Actually, the photograph was taken just outside the Smithsons' house in Limerston Street in Chelsea. Alison Smithson is on a tubular steel cantilever chair. Maybe it's a Marcel Breuer design, though it's hard to tell from the picture; more likely it's the low-cost British version made by Practical Equipment Ltd (PEL). Henderson himself and Peter Smithson are both seated on Charles and Ray Eames chairs, Smithson on a DSR fibreglass side chair, with the so-called Eiffel Tower steel-rod legs. It was designed in 1950, making it among the first examples to be imported to Britain. Henderson's is an LAR armchair. Paolozzi seems impaled atop a high wooden stool – an unsmiling, truculent Caliban. It was an image that created a template for vinyl album covers and suggested that something undefinable but certainly culturally important was at last beginning to happen against the essentially frivolous cultural backdrop of the England of the Festival of Britain.

It was also an epitaph of a kind for the group: the Smithsons had completed Hunstanton School the previous year, their tribute to Mies van der Rohe in Norfolk, and were soon going to be too busy building the Economist and their blocks of

A changing display of work by Kasmin's artists hung on the walls of the Neal Street Restaurant

flats in the East End for much more aesthetic speculation. Paolozzi and Henderson moved out of London to Thorpe-le-Soken in Essex and set up Hammer Prints to make fabrics, wallpaper and ceramics together.

By 1969, Terence had moved from the edge of the conversation to centre stage. He met Kasmin – who, after leaving Victor Musgrave's Gallery One and spending time running the Marlborough's New London Gallery, opened his own gallery on New Bond Street. Kasmin had begun life as John Kaye, then renamed himself John Kasmin, and finally dropped his first name. Thanks to an investment from Sheridan Hamilton-Temple-Blackwood, the fifth and last Marquess of Dufferin and Ava, known more simply as Sheridan Dufferin, Kasmin was able to commission Richard Burton to design a space that provided an impressive setting for a series of head-turning exhibitions. He started in 1963 with the colour-field work of Kenneth Noland, and followed it with David Hockney's first one-man show. Kasmin also represented Barnett Newman, Frank Stella, Anthony Caro, Richard Smith, Robyn Denny and Howard Hodgkin.

Terence and Kasmin – working with Christina Smith, Terence's former assistant who had moved to Neal Street in 1961, and who had gradually taken over many of Covent Garden's empty properties – opened Garage, an impressive new contemporary art gallery, in 1973. For a moment it showed the potential to trigger the emergence of another generation of artists. Though it did not last long enough to do so, it was nevertheless a significant experiment. Garage was the product of a deepening friendship between Terence, Caroline Herbert, who had become his third wife, and Kasmin. It began with a shared love of fine Burgundy and inventive cooking. On holiday in France in the summer of 1970, they planned the opening of a restaurant together in Neal Street, with Oliver Gregory, a long-standing lieutenant of Terence's, as a third partner. Kasmin and Gregory had ten per cent of the shares each; Terence, who funded the project, had the rest.

Terence had recently moved his offices to a building on Neal Street, controlled by Christina Smith, which had an empty ground-floor space that they leased for what they simply called the Neal Street Restaurant. The restaurant had a street front designed by the architect Max Clendinning for a project initiated by Smith which was never realised. In the interests of economy, Terence, Gregory and Keith Hobbs, a young designer in the Conran Studio, kept the facade in place painted a deep blue, and behind it created an intimate sixty-four-seat restaurant on the ground floor with a bar in the basement. David Hockney designed the menu, there were Frank Stella prints on the buttermilk-coloured walls, recessed downlighters in the ceiling, cream-coloured clay tiles on the floor and Thonet bentwood chairs at the tables. You passed a marble-topped shelf full of bowls of

David Hockneys favourite meal

Beluga Caviare

Watercress Soup   Truite au

Châteaubriands Sauce Béarnaise

Mange tout   haricots vert.

Cheese

Creme Brulée

no coffee (it is a killer)

Gerwertzraminer.
Château Lafitte
Château Yquem

TERENCE CONRAN   MAKING MODERN BRITAIN

AN EDUCATION IN ARTS AND CRAFTS

Kasmin asked David Hockney to create an image for the Neal Street Restaurant's menu. The original used to hang behind the reception, along with Hockney's personal recommendation. By the standards of Quaglino's, the restaurant was of a modest scale, but it quickly established itself as the place to go for the art world

Garage, the pioneering Covent Garden gallery, across the road from the Neal Street Restaurant, lasted from 1973 to 1975

food as you came in. Behind it hung the framed Hockney painting that was used for the menu design, and, for a while, a list of the artist's recommendations on what to order. The cutlery was designed by David Mellor. The restaurant featured an impressive multi-tiered service station made from chromed steel and marble. It was photographed for the 1971 Habitat catalogue, along with images of Kasmin's gallery in New Bond Street.

The next step was for Terence, Kasmin and Christina Smith to open the gallery across the street. For Smith it was a piece of enlightened self-interest. Covent Garden's vegetable market was in its last days on the building it had occupied since 1832 as it prepared to move to a new building at Nine Elms, south of the river. The Greater London Council (GLC) was planning a wholesale redevelopment that would involve demolishing several hundred buildings in the area, and the building of a new road layout. The campaign against this destructive scheme was a turning point in the history of planning in London. Until the battle for Covent Garden it was generally accepted in Britain that big plans represented certainly inevitable, and probably desirable, progress. Inspired by Jane Jacobs's earlier campaign to stop the destruction of Greenwich Village by the planned construction of a highway through New York's West Side, a network of activists started fighting against the GLC's proposals to destroy what they knew could become a thriving and attractive creative community.

Terence and Smith agreed with them, and had the idea of opening a new gallery as a chance to demonstrate how the area could be reused.

In 1971, the streets of Covent Garden were still dominated by wholesale fruit and vegetable dealers, their employees pushing trolleys of produce back and forth to their stores. But they were moving out. There were very few shop windows, just roller shutters that were mostly painted green. The Middle Earth club had set up a few years earlier in a basement in King Street, offering a diet of light shows, Pink

Floyd and Soft Machine. The area was still geared to the needs of the early hours working of the market. In those days of strict licensing controls, Covent Garden was a place in which pubs were allowed to open at dawn, to allow the market workers to order a pint of Guinness to go with their breakfast fry-up. The Opera House was the other big presence in the area. It meant that there were some streets where you could see musical instrument suppliers amid the fruit stalls. It was a snapshot of a city that was about to change out of all recognition.

Garage was at 52 Earlham Street in a building controlled by Smith, in which Terence used to park his Porsche on his way to the office. Terence talked about the idea of an art gallery with Kasmin. With his own gallery in New Bond Street to run, Kasmin was not going to open another place to show his own artists' work. Why not, he suggested, make a gallery for work from a younger generation of artists with less obvious commercial appeal?

An advisory group of artists including Caro and Hockney was established which gave the project unusual credibility, Terence's team refurbished the space, and two curators, Anthony Stokes and Martin Attwood, were appointed as co-directors.

Garage lasted less than two years from 1973 to 1975, but it helped to trigger a change of heart about the area. The Environment Minister, Geoffrey Rippon, listed 200 buildings in Covent Garden, which was made a conservation area. For the first time in Britain a popular campaign had stopped a large-scale masterplan. It was the start of a period of reflection and reassessment among Britain's planners and architects, which produced a new approach to urban development based on reuse and renovation rather than a clean slate – one that Terence would later take to Butler's Wharf. It was one of the triggers for the loss of faith in modernism and the idea of progress that took place in the second half of the 1970s. New was no longer automatically taken to mean better.

Turning Covent Garden into a conservation area where the existing buildings had a long-term future had the unforeseen consequence of raising their value considerably, pushing rents beyond what an experimental gallery could afford. It was the start of a process that took Covent Garden from market traders to the counterculture, and then to the super-fashionable, until the area was hollowed out by the dulling effect of too much success, and too much aimless mass tourism.

Garage never had a single guiding vision; some of the exhibitions went over Terence's head. But years later he did understand that Garage might have been a forerunner of the White Cube. It had, for example, staged the first professionally presented all-female group show of contemporary artists that London had ever seen, when the Royal College of Art pulled out of its original commitment to show it, and the Arts Council turned it down. Titled *c. 7,500*, for the population of Valencia, the small town in California from which it originated, it was organised by the American curator Lucy Lippard, and showed the work of twenty-six female conceptual artists, including the then unknown Laurie Anderson. When the Royal College of Art pulled out, and the Arts Council would not help, Garage stepped in.

But when the Habitat catalogue offered specially commissioned prints from what it called 'four of Britain's most important artists, all at £3 a print, all at the RCA in the vintage years', Terence and his partner in the project, Bernie Jacobson, selected Dick Smith, Robyn Denny, Peter Blake and Hockney, rather than more radical newcomers. Editions of Smith's *Sun Curtain* are now advertised for sale at £850. An example of Blake's print of his daughter, Liberty, wearing a kimono was acquired by the V&A from Jacobsen Conran Ltd in 1972. In any case, Terence's career was already moving away from the world of art, into the mainstream of business.

[1] Nicholas Ind, *Terence Conran: The Authorised Biography* (London: Sidgwick & Jackson, 1995).
[2] British Library, 'Terence Conran interviewed by Linda Sandino', in *National Life Stories* (London, 2004-5).
[3] Ibid.
[4] Fiona MacCarthy, 'Donald Potter', *The Guardian* (8 June 2004), www.theguardian.com/news/2004/jun/08/guardianobituaries.artsobituaries [Accessed 15 September 2021].
[5] Ibid.
[6] Terence Conran, *Printed Textile Design* (London: Studio Publications, 1957), 52.
[7] Ibid.
[8] In conversation with the author.
[9] JM Richards (ed.), *Architectural Review*, 112/668 (1952), 127. Quoted in Anne Massey and Gregor Muir (eds.), *ICA 1946-68* (London: ICA, 2014), 77.
[10] Toni del Renzio, *Art News and Review* (1953), 6.

Working for other people

TERENCE CONRAN MAKING MODERN BRITAIN

Terence did well at the Central School. He was already selling his designs as a student alongside much better-established designers such as Lucienne Day, who was born in 1917. She was perhaps the most original and successful textile designer of her generation, to whose work Terence owed a certain debt. David Whitehead & Sons Ltd – an old, established Lancashire textile company that was investing in new machinery – had appointed a young architect, John Murray, rather than a traditional pattern buyer to look for new designers. He found Terence in a selling exhibition of student designs organised by the Central School, and the two became friends. By 1949 Terence's design, Chequers, was in production with Whitehead. Terence sold designs to Edinburgh Weavers, the innovative company set up by Alastair Morton – who was an artist himself, and who, from 1930 onward, worked with a number of distinguished artists including Ben Nicholson, Barbara Hepworth and designers such as Enid Marx, Ashley Havinden and Lucienne Day. Terence also sold work to Horrocks, a textile firm that made cotton prints for mainstream women's fashion.

It was these early successes that helped Terence decide to leave art school in the summer of 1949 without completing his course. He had been offered a job by the architect Dennis Lennon, director of the newly established Rayon Design Centre. Before making up his mind about accepting it, Terence went to see Dora Batty in her room at the Central School. She was supportive and sympathetic, and advised him to take a job with a high-profile organisation and a salary, rather than take a risk trying to make it on his own with no more than a diploma in textile design.

With his well-cut Savile Row suits, his Triumph sports car and a persuasive manner, Lennon seemed the embodiment of a suave, faintly raffish architect of the 1940s. He knew everybody, from John Murray at Whitehead, to Elsbeth and Hans Juda of *The Ambassador* magazine and Theo Crosby, the South African born architect who organised *This is Tomorrow* at the Whitechapel Gallery, and later became a partner at the Pentagram design consultancy. Lennon had been a dashing war hero, spending three months on the run in German-occupied France in 1940 before escaping through Spain to reach Gibraltar. Acting Captain Lennon went on to win a Military Cross for gallantry at the Battle of El Alamein. According to the

Max Fry and Jane Drew were post-war Britain's best-connected architects

Fry worked with Walter Gropius in the 1930s. Together with Drew, he formed a partnership with Le Corbusier to build Chandigarh, the Punjab's new state capital

citation, he set an example to his men by helping to destroy twenty-four enemy tanks. Lennon had studied architecture at the Bartlett School, part of University College London, before joining the Royal Engineers in 1939. The Bartlett was led by Sir Albert Richardson, one of the founders of the Georgian Society, and a firm believer in Beaux-Arts' teaching methods. Students were expected to be able to learn to draw the classical orders with the aid of an elaborate array of compasses and set squares, and use them as the base for composing academically correct facades, carefully rendered in watercolour and with cast shadows.

Despite such a firmly traditional architectural education, Lennon joined Maxwell Fry and Jane Drew's practice soon after demobilisation. This was the most high-profile and best-connected modernist practice in London. Fry had been Walter Gropius's partner in London for three years before the founder of the Bauhaus left Britain for America. After the war, Fry and Drew formed an alliance with Le Corbusier to build Chandigarh, a new capital for the Punjab, after the partition of India and Pakistan that was one of the consequences of Britain's withdrawal. It was an unbeatable combination that, for a while, made the two of them the gate-keepers of modernism in Britain. Drew made possible Le Corbusier's exhibition of paintings, drawings, sculpture and tapestries at the Institute of Contemporary Arts (ICA) in 1953. Fry and Drew went into partnership with Denys Lasdun, who was able to build a much more lyrical version of British modernism than his partners. Nevertheless, these were connections that made Fry and Drew's Gloucester Place studio a crucial centre for architecture in London in the 1940s and 1950s. They designed universities, hospitals and technical colleges for Britain's remaining colonies, and headquarters' buildings for self-consciously progressive companies in England. Significantly, the studio letterhead styled itself as 'The Office of Maxwell Fry & Jane Drew Architects, Town Planners and Industrial Designers' – an echo of how Charles and Ray Eames presented themselves.

Fry and Drew worked on the *Britain Can Make It* exhibition at the V&A in 1946, and so were the natural choice to be appointed as the architects for the Rayon Design Centre when it was set up in 1948. The centre was an organisation established by Harold Wilson, president of the Board of Trade in the Attlee Government, with financial support from the textile industry. It was part of a drive towards economic regeneration to make British manufacturers more competitive. The objective was to promote rayon as a premium product, to overcome the negative connotations of its reputation among potential customers as 'artificial silk'. As an artificial fibre, rayon was seen as technologically advanced, much like lithium-ion battery factories are today. Manufacturing it offered Britain's industries a competitive advantage, and a direction for the future.

Dennis Lennon became the director of the Rayon Design Centre after helping Jane Drew to design its interior

WORKING FOR OTHER PEOPLE

The Rayon Design Centre set out to transform the public image of the material and persuade manufacturers to make better use of design

The centre took over a grand eighteenth-century Mayfair townhouse, full of elaborate plasterwork, at 1 Upper Grosvenor Street. Lennon worked as Drew's assistant to adapt the building to its new use, and he commissioned Jacqueline Groag, a former student of Josef Hoffmann in Vienna who had come to London as a refugee in 1939, to help him with the colour scheme.

In the course of designing the project, Lennon was offered the role of director at the centre. He left Fry and Drew and recruited a small team to work for him. Terence's job, as Lennon's assistant, was to keep the centre looking stylish and to run its programme of exhibitions that targeted both the public and industry. The centre aimed to set up a virtuous circle: the manufacturers were encouraged to come up with more interesting fabric designs, which could be used to make more enticing displays for the public, and so stimulate the demand for rayon textiles. The greater the demand, the more manufacturers could see the benefits that came from working with designers.

Terence made some of the furniture for the centre, designed the changing displays and bought the flowers to decorate the reception desk – as it happened, they came from Constance Spry's nearby shop. The florist, who was the subject of an exhibition at the Design Museum many years later that caused Terence to question the judgement of its director, had her shop Flower Decoration around the corner on South Audley Street. In his account of design in post-war Britain, Michael Farr wrote of the Rayon Design Centre:

Furnished throughout with modern designs of a high standard, it was the first place to take foreign visitors, who wanted to see some of the best examples of British industrial art in actual use, a register of available designers, a reference collection of fabrics from abroad, small but enticing exhibitions in its own display room.[1]

With no more experience of editorial work than designing the cover of the Bryanston school magazine, Terence put together the three issues of *Rayon and Design*, a glossy magazine published by the centre to put its message across. It had lush production values and had as much to say about design as it did about rayon. The magazine gave Terence a platform and the chance to meet influential people. He interviewed Hardy Amies, among others. He also published his own work and designed the very striking covers. Volume 1, Issue 1, was dated December 1949. 'I did the drawings, I interviewed a lot of fashion designers and I showed my work. I think it was Amies who called one of my designs "hideous and repellent",' Terence recalled.[2] Drew also makes an appearance in the magazine,

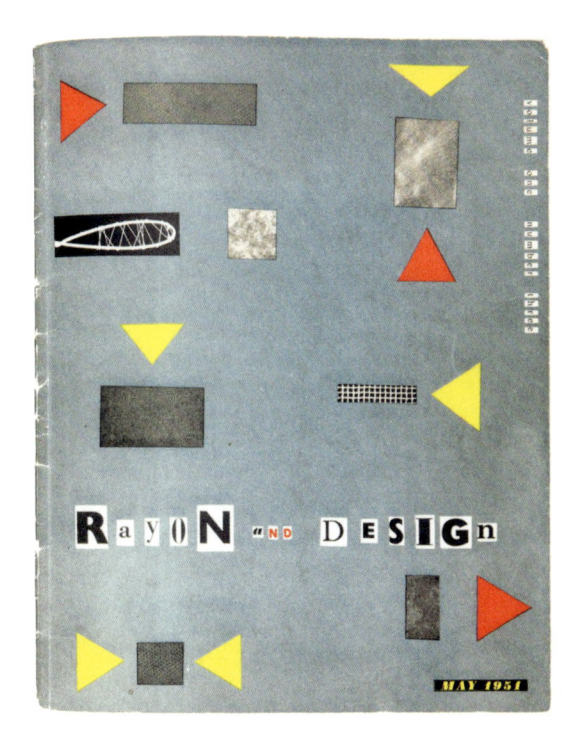

The last of the three issues of the *Rayon and Design* magazine that Terence had art-directed

joining Amies as part of a panel providing a commentary on contemporary textile designs. Inspired by the Central School's selling show, a range of designers, including Terence himself, was commissioned by Lennon to produce designs that were subsequently sold to manufacturers and put into production.

And when *The Ambassador* magazine, published by his friends Hans and Elsbeth Juda, later sponsored an exhibition at the ICA of painting on textiles, Whitehead bought from six of the twenty-five artists involved. Looking back at the period, Terence wrote: 'David Whitehead and its executive Dr John Murray saved my professional life in 1949 by buying some of my textile designs; they did the same for a few other designers who could find no outlet for their creative energies.'[3]

Three years after the Rayon Design Centre opened, a newly elected Conservative government took a less interventionist approach to economic policy than its Labour predecessor, and shut it down. The building was demolished not long after, in the 1950s, to make way for Eero Saarinen's American Embassy on Grosvenor Square.

Lennon opened his own architectural practice in Manchester Square in 1950, where Terence worked as his assistant. It was while he was working there that Lennon once persuaded Terence to join him on a walk across the square to the Wallace Collection that stands on the north side of Oxford Street. But Lennon

The Ridgeway Hotel in Lusaka, in what was then Northern Rhodesia and is now Zambia, opened in 1951. Dennis Lennon designed the interior, Terence produced a number of chairs for the bar, including this one, upholstered in a fabric designed by Eduardo Paolozzi

failed to interest Terence in its lavishly ornamental display of eighteenth-century French furniture.

Although Lennon did design a number of major buildings, he was better known for his interiors, and built a successful practice with more of a concentration on interior design than was common for architects in Britain at that time. When the catering giant J Lyons & Co. wanted to modernise its Corner House restaurants, and pension off the waitresses it dressed in black alpaca and called 'nippies', it was Dennis Lennon who got the job of transforming thirty-seven of the restaurants into London Steak Houses. He gave each of them its own character, all of them confidently contemporary, with art on the walls and Hans Wegner dining chairs. Lennon also designed glossy-looking fashion stores for Jaeger starting in the 1950s, in locations all the way from Glasgow to Nassau.

It was Lennon who led the design team working on the interiors of the Cunard liner *QE2*, a ship that for a while exemplified modern Britain. Over the course of his career, he designed hotels, clubs and entertainments, including a gala night at the Royal Opera House for the Shah of Iran. The V&A has a couple of pieces of furniture that he designed in its collection. It was a particular range and flavour of projects, which created a template that Terence would follow when he set up a design studio of his own.

While Terence still worked for him, Lennon secured a commission in Lusaka, the capital of what was then called Northern Rhodesia, and is now Zambia. The Ridgeway Hotel was designed by Geoffrey Jellicoe, with Lennon responsible for the interiors. Terence designed the hotel's more informal furniture, upholstered in fabrics he hand-printed from designs by Paolozzi. Lennon designed some rather bulkier armchairs, equipped with decorative brass ferrules. The Council of Industrial Design exhibited the whole range in London at its Petty France offices.

Terence worked with Lennon on the transformation of a tailor's shop on Shepherd's Place in Mayfair into the Café Boulevard, which mixed strong colour with the decorative prints that he would soon apply to his own restaurants, as well as to the Partas brassiere showroom in the West End. In addition to his ability to find clients, Lennon had a gift for identifying talented assistants. After hiring Terence he gave David Mlinaric a job, which was the start of Mlinaric's successful career as an interior designer. Lennon was also responsible for introducing Terence to another of his employees, Brenda Davison. She was a recent architecture graduate from Cambridge, who would briefly become Terence's first wife – a relationship that broke down within a few months of their register-office wedding in 1952 and ended in divorce in 1954.

Britain in the years after the war was going through a period of profound change, even if many of those in power failed to notice. Its political leaders still believed that Britain was a great imperial power with a global role, the peer of the US and the USSR. The country developed its own nuclear weapon, which it detonated for the first time in 1952 on the Montebello Islands in Western Australia. It took a leading role in the establishment of the United Nations and NATO. It was a major trading nation, thanks to the colonial trading bloc linked to sterling. Culturally, many of Britain's elite believed that it could afford to continue to view the modernism of Picasso and Le Corbusier with faintly condescending disdain. The elite's view followed that of James Manson, the pre-war director of the Tate Gallery. He had refused to exhibit Henry Moore – 'over my dead body', as he put it.[4] The elite agreed, albeit in more temperate terms than the dipsomaniac Manson

David Lennon's interior drawing for the Partas showroom

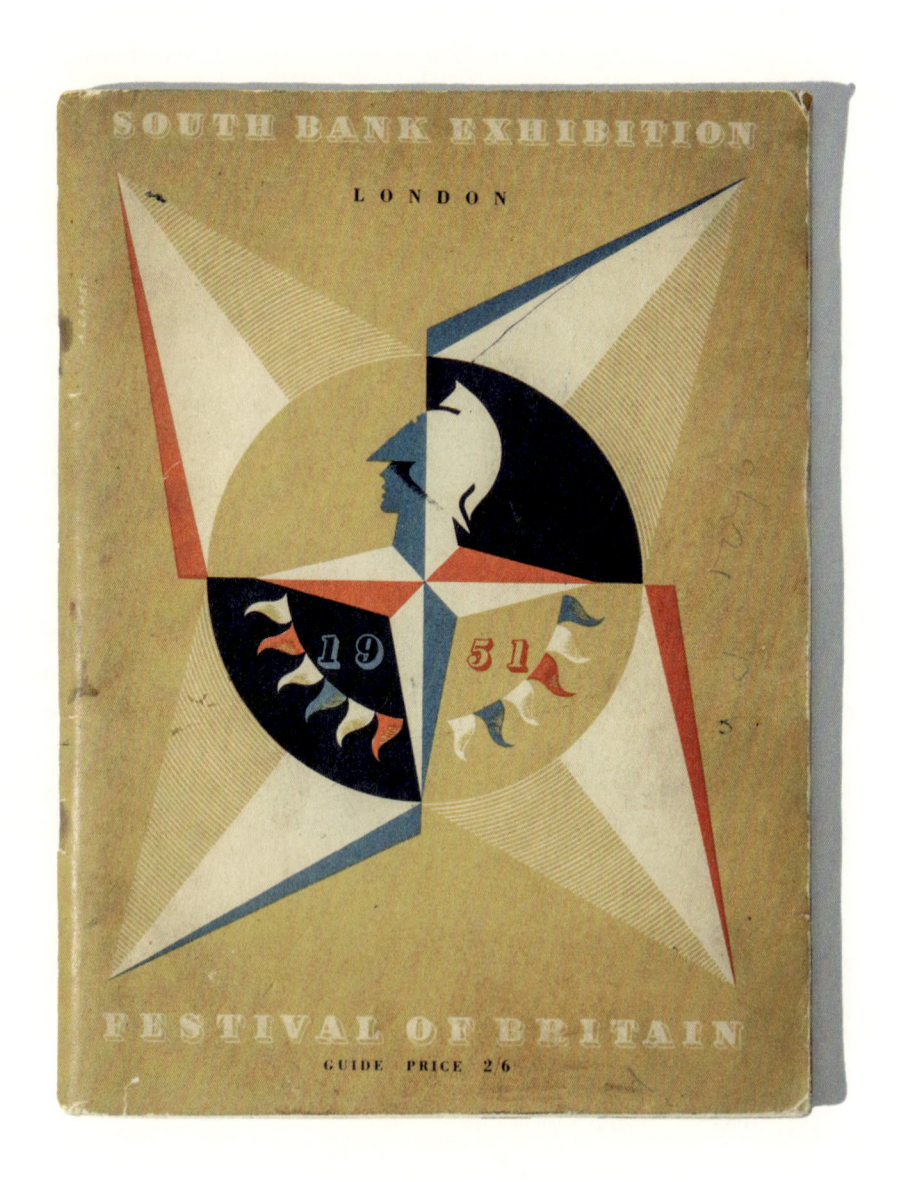

Abram Games's symbol for the Festival of Britain combined Britannia and a star

who, when asked as late as 1938 to certify a consignment of sculptures belonging to Peggy Guggenheim on the way from France to be exhibited as art in her London gallery, and so exempt from import duty, refused to do so. Constantin Brancusi's *Sculpture for the Blind* was not art at all, Manson declared, before being forced to back down by a public outcry.

In fact, Britain was politically and economically vulnerable, completely dependent on America, as its humiliation over the invasion of Egypt in an attempt to undo the nationalisation of the Suez Canal demonstrated in 1956. Culturally it depended on a wave of refugees from mainland Europe for much of its creative energy. And as the Tate episode showed, Britain was in danger of becoming an insular backwater. Peggy Guggenheim changed her mind about gifting her collection to London. Initially the Festival of Britain – the event that had overshadowed the thinking of every architect and designer in Britain since Gerald Barry, editor of the *News Chronicle*, had made the case for it to the Labour government in 1947 – was meant to address that insularity. Barry incidentally employed the very young Paul Reilly as a journalist who, by the time of the Festival, would join the Council for Industrial Design, later becoming the director of the Design Council, and, as Lord Reilly, first chair of Terence's charity, the Conran Foundation. His life was commemorated with a plaque at the entrance to the old Design Museum at Shad Thames. Barry echoed a paper put forward by the Royal Society of Arts during the war, which proposed marking the centenary of the Great Exhibition of 1851 with an international world's fair.

A post-war sterling crisis in 1947 followed by a second in 1949 that saw the pound crash from $4.03 to $2.80, together with the start of the war in Korea, threatened to kill off the Festival altogether. It survived, reduced in scope and ambition, as a celebration of British identity. Barry suggested that 'the Festival of Britain is intended to be a corporate act of national reassessment, and of a reaffirmation of our faith in the future.' It would, he insisted, be 'a year of fun, fantasy and colour, a year in which we can, while soberly surveying our great past and our promising future, for once let ourselves go.'[5]

As things turned out, while it might not have produced the most innovative examples of contemporary design in the world, the Festival's budget for consultancy fees and its staff jobs helped to sustain London's architects and designers for three difficult years. Between May and October of 1951, the Festival of Britain's main site attracted more than eight million visitors.

Hugh Casson often claimed that the Festival was seen politically as the creation of a Labour regime, and that when Churchill and the Conservative Party returned to power in October 1951 they immediately set about wiping out all traces

Hugh Casson, director of architecture for the Festival of Britain

Misha Black from the Design Research Unit

of the event. In fact, there is little evidence for that having been the case. It is hard to overstate how comprehensively the Festival embraced the British establishment. Barry reported to a Festival Council chaired by General Lord Ismay, Churchill's chief military advisor during the war, afterwards becoming NATO's first secretary general. Members included Kenneth Clark, director of the National Gallery, TS Eliot, John Gielgud and Sir Malcolm Sargent. According to the Churchill scholar Iain Wilton, there is no documented source for the claim that Churchill called the festival 'three-dimensional socialist propaganda'.[6] In fact, Churchill lent the corrected proof of his wartime memoirs to the festival exhibition. And demolition of the pavilions on the South Bank began in the closing weeks of a Labour administration, not as the opening act of a Conservative one. Only the Festival Hall remains.

Barry was appointed director general in March 1948, with an executive committee made up of appointees from the Arts Council, the Council for Industrial Design and the British Film Institute. He was allocated a site between County Hall and Waterloo Bridge that was both more difficult to work with and smaller than the one in Hyde Park that he had hoped for. It was cut in two by a railway viaduct and, to complicate matters, was not in single ownership. It was also partly covered in a mountain of bomb-damaged rubble and, with no embankment in place on the riverbank, trailed away into tidal mud. Though the site was mainly derelict, before work could start the former White Lion brewery would have to be demolished.

A masterplan for the Festival was prepared by a group of five architects and designers made up of Misha Black, Ralph Tubbs, James Holland, James Gardner

WORKING FOR OTHER PEOPLE

The Festival site was split in two by the railway lines from Charing Cross. The Dome of Discovery and the Skylon were upstream, with the Festival Hall to the east, designed by a team from the London County Council's architecture department led by Robert Matthew, Leslie Martin and Peter Moro

Misha Black, James Holland, Ralph Tubbs and Hugh Casson, key members of the team that planned the Festival of Britain and had also designed some of the major pavilions. Tubbs was responsible for the Dome of Discovery; Casson repurposed a nineteenth-century shot tower, and made a pavilion devoted to the Great Exhibition

Powell and Moya's Skylon, the only major commission for the Festival of Britain to be allocated through an open competition. The needle-thin monument, 300 feet high, was suspended 50 feet above the ground

and Hugh Casson. 'We used to meet in an attic bedroom of a requisitioned house off Sloane Street huddled in overcoats, we sat hour after hour, the tracing paper piled up around our knees,' Casson remembered. They began work in September 1948. The masterplan was approved by Christmas, and the briefs for the individual pavilions went out in March 1949.

To add to the insularity of the Festival, just two of its projects were selected by open competition: the Skylon, Powell and Moya's needle-like tribute to Constructivism that was hoisted fifty feet off the ground by a web of cables and rose to almost three hundred feet, and Leonard Manasseh's 1951 restaurant. Casson allocated everything else to a limited collection of architects without ever specifying any criteria for the selections that he made. It is notable, however, that Casson, James Gardner, Dick Russell and Robert Goodden had all served together during the war in the Admiralty's Camouflage Unit and would all work at the Festival. According to Dick Negus, who worked on the exhibition display, Basil Spence picked the commission to design the Ships and the Sea pavilion out of a hat. Spence was a major in the Royal Artillery's camouflage section.

Set against the kind of work by Charles and Ray Eames and the Case Study houses that Terence was seeing in *Arts & Architecture*, the magazine that started publishing in California in 1945, and *Domus*, edited by Gio Ponti in Milan with its bravura art direction, much of what the Festival came up with architecturally looked provincial or gratingly whimsical. But in its graphic design and exhibition displays it was more impressive.

In the run-up to the opening in 1951, while he was still running the Rayon Design Centre, Lennon worked with the Festival Pattern Group, which was exploring the creation of a new language of decorative pattern-making based on scientific motifs. This was an initiative by Mark Hartland Thomas, the Council of Industrial Design's chief industrial officer, who set up an experiment to work with a range

The Transport pavilion, designed by Rodney Thomas of Arcon, had three full-size aircraft suspended from its roof, contained within a glass-fronted space at the front of the structure

FHK Henrion, the graphic designer who recruited Terence to work on the displays for the Countryside pavilion, made his reputation with wartime posters

of designers commissioned to produce patterns based on crystal structures and molecules of various kinds, as a modern alternative to the leaf and flower patterns of traditional decoration.

Lennon introduced the textile manufacturers who backed the Rayon Design Centre to the group, and they agreed to make textiles using the new patterns. The Regatta Restaurant on the South Bank, designed by Misha Black and Alexander Gibson, was used to showcase them during the Festival. Surprisingly, however, Lennon failed to get a major design commission for the Festival of Britain, even though his former employers Fry and Drew got to do three buildings: the New Schools pavilion, the Thameside Restaurant and the Festival administration's offices. Ralph Tubbs, who had also worked for Fry, was handed the Dome of Discovery.

Lennon did do some rather more modest work with Terence inside the Transport pavilion, designed by the architect Rodney Thomas. A largely forgotten figure today, Thomas was responsible for several striking interiors in the 1930s, and in the post-war years he designed the successful Arcon prefabricated house. Thomas gave the pavilion a tilted glass front that revealed a cluster of full-size aircraft, two gliders and a Supermarine Swift, slung from the roof inside, apparently in the middle of a steep dive. Lennon and Conran worked on a large-scale model of the Princess flying boat, then being built by Saunders-Roe. The Princess did not make its maiden flight until the following year, but the company was keen to show off the potential of this monster with ten turboprop engines, a 240-foot wingspan, a pressurised metal hull, and a double-deck layout capable of accommodating up to two hundred passengers.

In fact, it would soon become clear that the Princess had no future. Landing on water rather than on a concrete runway was too dangerous, even if it might

John Piper's mural *The Englishman's Home* for the Homes pavilion, 1951

Inside Bronek Katz's Homes and Gardens pavilion were six specially designed interiors

seem convenient, and a salt-filled atmosphere made the airframe too vulnerable to corrosion. The flying boat era was already over, but the Festival was not in the business of puncturing illusions. Terence helped to install the model and decorated its interior. It looked like an impressive glimpse of the future, even if it was actually a dinosaur.

Terence moonlighted as an assistant on other projects on the site, including working for FHK Henrion, a graphic designer born in Germany who moved to Paris before setting up his studio in London in 1936. Henrion produced memorable wartime propaganda posters and became a pioneer of corporate identity. He was responsible for the displays in two pavilions, the Country and the Natural Scene, both of them built by Brian O'Rorke, an architect from New Zealand best known for the interiors of the liner *Oriana*. Terence made some of the signage, and he was also able to show some of his textiles in the Home pavilion designed by Bronek Katz and curated by the Council of Industrial Design.

The Home pavilion had perhaps the most clearly articulated message of all the displays. It talked about space and certainly spoke to Terence. Consciously or not, it did a lot to shape his thinking about the nature of domestic life. On the eve of a massive house-building programme, in which new housing starts would reach 300,000 a year (a figure that present-day Britain is nowhere near repeating), the Council was lecturing the British public about how precious space is. The Council was also attempting to show how designers and architects could help make the most of it.

The pavilion opened with an information graphic showing the price of a square foot of building land, in both pounds sterling and a variety of international currencies. It missed a chance to draw a comparison between prices in cities with wildly differing densities. The accompanying text, interrupted with staccato messages in all capitals for extra urgency, read:

> *Fifty million people crowd this country, four out of five live in towns. Space in towns is limited and costly, the key to homemaking is the use of space. In this pavilion you will see how we in Britain are trying to solve some of the problems of the home.*

> *Increasing demands on space and the rising costs of building have led to smaller houses and smaller rooms. A sense of freedom in the home can be achieved by forming zones for various activities and dividing these by easily movable screens, curtains and folding walls.*

Sitting room plus dining room plus kitchen

EQUALS MORE LIVING SPACE

The layout shows how in making the living, dining and kitchen subdivisions of one unit, spaciousness can still be maintained; and the housewife can take part in the social life of the home while working in the kitchen. A supply of constant hot water saves space and labour. The problem of saving space in the kitchen is largely the problem of storage.

The kitchen zone is designed to do away with all unnecessary movement. The utility room is kept separate FOR REASONS OF HYGIENE AND EFFICIENCY.[7]

Other exhibits in the pavilion included a timeline documenting the evolution of cookers, sinks, irons and kettles. It was shown alongside displays of light fittings, suspended over a working demonstration of how to light a living room for different occasions. Most striking were the room sets. A selection of designers was commissioned to produce a concept for a living space that would reflect the life of its user. The results were realised as a sequence of sets furnished, lit, decorated and presented as shop-window exhibits.

Robin Day became one of the best known of the designers who worked on the individual room interiors. These were designed to reflect the needs and tastes of specific though imaginary users, from growing children to 'elderly spinsters'. There was a 'country parlour' designed by Frank Austin and Neville Ward, and a 'town parlour' with pieces designed by Gordon Russell. It featured non-utility furniture manufactured using Nigerian cherry – something of a sensation after years of rationing, which limited the sale of new furniture to the bombed-out and the newly married, and then only government-approved 'utility' designs were available. Utility represented all the principles of good design as promoted by the Council of Industrial Design: logical, economical and stripped of unnecessary ornament. These items had the predictable effect of inoculating a generation against 'good design', which was inevitably associated with the scarcities and deprivation of rationing. The 'town parlour' had storage units made by Hille, and a sofa and aluminium chairs designed by Ernest Race. The 'bed sitting room for an elderly maiden lady' had another Ernest Race piece: a rocking chair.

The 'Entertainment at Home' exhibit from the Home pavilion was designed by Robin Day, with sculptures by Barbara Hepworth and Reg Butler on the sideboard,

WORKING FOR OTHER PEOPLE

Visitors to the Homes and Gardens pavilion saw six different room sets

Robin Day's room set for the Homes and Gardens pavilion looked at entertainment in the home

Brian O'Rorke was responsible for the architecture of the Country pavilion, and Henrion designed the displays. Visitors could see a selection of live farm animals, as well as a cluster of modern tractors apparently floating in space

a Murphy radio and a working TV set in front of a sectional seating system designed for TV viewing – a sight so unusual that it created a bottleneck as crowds gathered to watch.

Terence had seen a similar approach at the *Britain Can Make It* exhibition with its room sets at the V&A five years before, and it would shape Terence's own techniques for selling furniture at Habitat in the 1960s. In fact, the guidance offered by Terence's enormously popular *House Book*, first published in 1974, echoed much of the Council for Industrial Design's advice on space-saving at the Festival.

For a nineteen-year-old, the six weeks spent working at the Festival, sometimes sleeping on site in a camp bed as the deadline for the public opening neared, were clearly a formative experience. It offered Terence the chance to feel that he was at the centre of an event that touched the whole country, and even to meet what seemed like every designer and architect of consequence in Britain, from Wells Coates, who designed the cinema, to Ralph Tubbs, architect of the Dome of Discovery – the 365-foot diameter structure that Hugh Casson, architecture director of the Festival, described as 'our Eiffel Tower'.

From the records of the Council of Industrial Design, it seems that was not a process that went entirely smoothly.

> *Urgent from Cecil Cooke the Director of Exhibitions. Chief causes of delay! 1. designer delay in selecting exhibits and photographs. I expressed grave concern about the position last November, since when it has steadily worsened. The bulk of the captioning has not been written or approved yet.*[8]

Contingency plans were made to send some of the typesetting work out of London, but Cooke doubted that provincial setters had either the capacity or the skill to handle it properly.

Michael Frayn called the Festival 'the triumph of Britain's herbivores over its carnivores'.[9] Certainly it was run by people who sounded like herbivores even if they ate meat. Miss Sydney Ford of the Council of Industrial Design wrote memos to her boss, Mr AD Hippisley-Coxe, who later retired to write books about sausages. Mr Morse-Brown was paid by the Council to run a series of lectures in the Homes and Gardens section after its research revealed that too many visitors were failing to understand the message. Mr Morse-Brown duly reported back:

I again spent my time trying to draw attention to the special design points which were being missed. No adverse criticism was heard other than the disappointment at not being able to know the cost of various articles. The design points were very well received although I had to emphasise the luxuriousness of the bed by suggesting that it was quite a good idea for an elderly lady to spend more money on her bed than on other articles of furniture. The restful colour schemes went over well. Note, the television sets were often the cause of traffic jams.

I suggest that we look at the question of security. The children's garden was alive with children, bashing the exhibits in a rather frightening manner, playing with transport toys, opening and slamming cooker and refrigerator doors etc.[10]

The Festival's exhibitions brought together Chippendale furniture and Rolls-Royce engines, paintings by Gainsborough, Constable and Turner, and the King James Bible. There were demonstrations by Brylcreemed craftsmen in collars and ties underneath their spotless white overalls, showing off their skills at making cricket bats and footballs. It depended on such quintessential figures of the time as Lady Lucas-Tooth, secretary of the Goldfish Society of Great Britain, from Westcliff-on-Sea in Essex, as well as the Surrey Beekeepers, the National Institute of Houseworkers and Lady Hart Dyke of the Lullingstone Silk Farm.

The Festival told its visitors all about blood transfusions and anaesthetics. It encouraged Graham Sutherland to get up a ladder with a paintbrush and Laurie Lee to write the brief for the Ships and the Sea pavilion. Abram Games devised the Festival Star. The signage, the litter bins, the chairs had all been designed by somebody. Ernö Goldfinger created the kiosks. Hugh Casson produced a menu in the form of a birdcage for the Aviary restaurant, designed a dais for the king and put on a top hat for the Festival opening ceremony. The Festival became inescapable. It even infected the advertising campaign for the Triumph Renown:

> *All that's best in Britain. At Bampton in Oxfordshire, the original traditional Morris dancing is still carried on, the fiddler, the dancers with the gay streamers carry us back to an age when every village was proud of its craftsmen. Our great national heritage which today finds its expression in the products of the Standard Motor Company representing as they do in every detail of their design all that's best in Britain.*[11]

But it wasn't long after the excitement had faded that Terence gave a more nuanced view of the significance of the event in his book *Printed Textile Design*, published in 1957.

> *Exhibitions which theoretically exert a good influence on design often do just the opposite. Manufacturers quickly realised the success of the 1951 Festival of Britain without understanding its essence. Their interpretations, which were aesthetically worthless but financially remunerative, bore no legitimate relation to that which they aped. And domestic design, especially printed fabric design, became increasingly decadent. However, for the first time since the Industrial Revolution (which completely changed the European economy and destroyed traditions of craftsmanship) the general public is taking an interest in good design and daily grows more discriminating.*[12]

He was not alone. James Stirling, as a young architect, wrote a piece for the *Architectural Review* in which he suggested that his response to the Festival was disgust. Casson, though only director of architecture for the Festival, and who managed to become its public face ahead of Gerald Barry and all the other designers and architects involved, was still bristling forty years later at suggestions that the event was the embodiment of the middle brow. 'We weren't high-brow, middle-brow or low-brow. We liked to be concertina-brow,' he claimed.[13]

By the time the Festival ended, Terence had decided that he was ready to build on the experiences of working for Lennon and his own activities in Paolozzi's workshop and set up for himself. He was ready for anything: designing, making, selling and even starting a restaurant.

[1] Michael Farr, *Design in British Industry: A Mid-Century Survey* (Cambridge: Cambridge University Press, 1955), 226-7.
[2] Nicholas Ind, *Terence Conran: The Authorised Biography* (London: Sidgwick & Jackson, 1995).
[3] Alan Peat, *David Whitehead Ltd: Artist Designed Textiles 1952-1969* (Oldham: Oldham Education & Leisure Services, 1993), 7.
[4] Frances Spalding, *The Tate: A History* (London: Tate Gallery Publishing, 1998), 62.
[5] Gerald Barry, 'At Home to the World,' *Come to Britain: A Survey by* The Times *in Cooperation with the British Travel and Holiday Association* (January 1951). Quoted in FM Leventhal, '"A Tonic to the Nation": The Festival of Britain, 1951', *Albion: A Quarterly Journal Concerned with British Studies*, 3/27 (Autumn 1995), 445-53.
[6] Iain Wilton, 'Winston Churchill and the 1951 Festival of Britain', *Finest Hour*, 174 (12 May 2017), winstonchurchill.org/publications/finest-hour/finest-hour-174/winston-churchill-and-the-1951-festival-of-britain/ [Accessed 16 September 2021].
[7] Design Council Archive, 'Festival of Britain 1946-53', *University of Brighton Design Archives* (1946-53), archiveshub.jisc.ac.uk/data/gb1837-des/dca/des/dca/14b [Accessed 16 September 2021].
[8] Ibid.
[9] Michael Frayn, 'Festival spirit', *The Guardian* (3 May 2001), www.theguardian.com/uk/2001/may/03/britishidentity.features11 [Accessed 16 September 2021].
[10] Design Council Archive
[11] Festival of Britain, *Festival of Britain, London: South Bank Exhibition, 1951* (London: HM Stationery Office, 1951).
[12] Terence Conran, *Printed Textile Design* (London: Studio Publications, 1957), 29.
[13] Hugh Casson, *National Life Story Collection Architects' Lives* (recorded lecture, 6 May 1991).

Working for himself

TERENCE CONRAN   MAKING MODERN BRITAIN

After the euphoria of the Festival of Britain had faded away, Terence left Dennis Lennon's studio to set up on his own, at what now seems the improbably young age of just twenty. Terence became the legal owner of his father's company, Conran and Co., in 1952. He used the company structure as a more formal business entity to manufacture and sell the furniture that he had been making informally for some years.

Work and life began to merge for Terence. Brenda Davison, whom Terence met at Lennon's office, told him that there was a room available to rent in the large, dilapidated house on Warwick Gardens, close to Kensington High Street, where she was living in exchange for helping to restore it. It belonged to Ivan Storey, a doctor friend of hers from when they had both been students at Cambridge. Storey, who had recently returned from military service in the war in Korea, had bought the house as a wreck and was letting out rooms to help him pay the mortgage.

Terence moved in while the house was still filling up with a colourful group of people, many of whom would help him take the next steps in his career in one way or another. Brenda and Terence got married, and she designed the catalogue for his first furniture collection the year before he opened the Orrery restaurant. She continued to buy his pieces for her own architectural projects even after they had separated.

Storey, Terence's landlord, would become his partner when together they started the Soup Kitchen restaurant in 1953. Den Newton, who was both a poet and an art critic making a living freelancing for architectural magazines (and who lived in the midst of his own personal cabinet of curiosities of what was then called 'primitive' art, which took up most of his room), wrote very positively about Terence's exhibition at Simpson, the Piccadilly menswear store, for the *Architectural Review*. Newton moved to New York in 1956, and spent the rest of his career at the Metropolitan Museum of Art as a curator of non-Western art.

Olive Sullivan, who had another room, worked for *House and Garden* magazine, and would be responsible for introducing him to the photographer Michael Wickham and his future wife Cynthia Blackburn when they came round one day to see her. Toby Jellinek, just out of his progressive boarding school education, was brought in by Terence and lived in the house for a while. He had helped Terence make his first pieces of furniture before leaving for the south of France with his girlfriend Sylvette David, where they encountered Picasso. Jellinek returned to Britain after his marriage to David failed, to become an antique dealer specialising in early English furniture.

Eduardo Paolozzi, who was renting a room nearby in Holland Road, became a fixture in the kitchen where he was locked in permanent conversation with Terence, whose room was too small to accommodate visitors and was equipped with furniture

Den Newton's room in the house that he shared with Terence

Terence's design for the first issue of *Nimbus*, a literary magazine from the 1950s that published poetry by Jean Cocteau and Christopher Logue

that he had made for himself. Terence and Paolozzi worked together in the kitchen on Paolozzi's plans for his exhibition at the ICA. A collage that Paolozzi made for Brenda during this period is a reminder of how close he, Terence and Brenda had once been.

Michael Wickham took Terence on a six-week odyssey through France in his vintage Lagonda in 1953, after the end of Terence's marriage to Brenda. This was the holiday that took on mythic status for Terence. It was the inspiration for so many of his ideas about retailing, which came from the generosity of the marketplaces of France, as well as confirming his taste for French food and wine. They ended up in the Dordogne, staying in a house owned by Nancy Cunard, the heiress who had known Ezra Pound and TS Eliot and had been the lover of Surrealist poet Louis Aragon.

Wickham photographed Terence's work for *House and Garden* when they first met, and he was still working for Habitat twenty-five years later. Terence's obituary for Wickham in *The Independent* painted a picture of a free-spending bohemian who loved food and wine, as much as Terence did himself, and who made the kitchen table at Barton Court for him. Terence is affectionate and wistful

The string and welded steel rod chair, a version of which Toby Jellinek made for Picasso

Colin St John Wilson, architect of the British Library, had a chair designed by Terence in his flat in the 1950s

in his tribute, and perhaps unwittingly presents Wickham as a much less driven, much less ambitious version of himself.

As Terence became closer to Brenda, the dynamic of life in the house in Warwick Gardens, where meals were shared around the table in the kitchen, changed. She left to live elsewhere. Newton and Terence both moved into Sloane Court West, close to the King's Road near Sloane Square. Nigel Henderson and his wife lived there too, having moved west from Bethnal Green. Their home was in part of a building that had been requisitioned during the war by the Auxiliary Territorial Service, the women's army, and left much the worse for wear by it. Henderson and

Terence was invited to design an exhibition of his work at Simpson, the department store in Piccadilly. Nigel Henderson photographed it, and Den Newton reviewed it for the *Architectural Review*

TERENCE CONRAN   MAKING MODERN BRITAIN

Natasha Kroll ran the display team at Simpson, and developed the store's reputation for experimentation. She went on to become a successful set designer for filmmakers

Terence both made studio workspaces for themselves there. Terence remembered the seriousness and commitment that Henderson brought to his work.

Terence's designs were already being showcased in some highly visible places very soon after he had started to work on his own. Natasha Kroll, the display manager for Simpson on Piccadilly, based in a building designed by Joseph Emberton, was one of the first to spot his talent. She asked him to create some window displays for the store. This led to her giving him the space for *Ideas and Objects for the Home* in 1952, an exhibition of his work at Simpson. It included examples of his chairs, storage units, tables and basketwork, put together as an impressive room set. This was a significant achievement for a twenty-year-old on more than one level. Terence was following in the footsteps of some major talents, not least László Moholy-Nagy, the Bauhaus artist, who was living in London when Simpson first opened in 1938.

Moholy-Nagy had been commissioned to fill a whole floor of the store with a display designed to celebrate the joy of flight. Moholy-Nagy installed three full-size aircraft, including the Pou du Ciel, a plane designed in France by Henri Mignet, as a simple way for 'anyone' to get into the air. It came in kit form and it could in theory be powered by a motorcycle engine. Moholy-Nagy displayed the planes as sculptural objects against a backdrop of his own photographs.

That Terence had impressed the formidable Kroll was also an achievement. Born in Moscow, educated in Berlin, Kroll became display manager at Simpson in 1942, and would later be celebrated as a designer for television and film, including the work she did for Ken Russell's account of Tchaikovsky's life, *The Music Lovers*.

Terence asked Henderson to photograph his exhibition at Simpson. Henderson's images were published in the *Architectural Review*, and the magazine's editor Ian McCallum, later the director of the American Museum in Bath, commissioned

The Simpson store used creative designers from the beginning. László Moholy-Nagy was commissioned to design an installation devoted to flight for the opening. It included three full-size aircraft, including the Pou du Ciel shown here

Terence to design furniture for his office and showed it to his friend the American architect Philip Johnson, on a visit to London. Johnson bought one of his chairs too.

Despite all this success, Terence was still very young, and still trying to find his place in the cultural landscape of London. He talked about how condescendingly the Smithsons behaved, but he felt much warmer about Henderson.

The Britain in which Terence set up in business on his own after leaving Lennon's office in 1952 was still a long way from being free of the restrictions introduced during the war. Food rationing would continue until the summer of 1954. Building materials were in short supply for even longer. For example, when the Commonwealth Institute, which would eventually become the Design Museum, was being designed at the start of the 1960s by RMJM, the choice of colours for the glass cladding panels was limited to plain grey or the slightly more cheerful option of pale turquoise blue. And after the war in 1947, the Exchange Control Act had put a strict limit on the amount of sterling currency that British travellers could take abroad, which made foreign travel difficult.

Terence, however, was undeterred. He became hyperactive in the face of the restrictions, starting new projects, opening workshops, hiring people and making bold new plans. He found a space for his first professional workshop in Notting Hill in the basement of the Mercury, a 150-seat theatre at 2 Ladbroke Road owned by Ashley Dukes, a playwright married to the ballet dancer Marie Rambert. The theatre put on Dukes's productions, and performances by the Rambert School of Ballet and Contemporary Dance. *The Red Shoes*, written, directed and produced by Powell and Pressburger, was filmed there. In the space underneath the theatre, Terence employed four people to weld steel rods to make chairs, tables and shelving, led by Eric O'Leary, who had previously assisted Henry Moore and made furniture for Henrion. When the Paolozzi terracotta tile was dropped on the floor,

O'Leary was skilled enough to be able to mend the damage without leaving a trace. The workshop was making Terence's S1 cabinet, with shelves and storage units supported by a welded steel frame, as well as an assortment of Conran's chairs. Like the Thonet bentwood furniture manufacture that he much admired, Terence used numbers, not names, for his products. In his catalogues Terence's storage designs were all coded with the letter S followed by a designating number in chronological order, while chairs were all designated with a C and a number.

But Terence needed a more accessible and appealing showroom than the subterranean space in remote Notting Hill could offer to reach the specifiers that made up his most important market. He found a basement in a florist's shop belonging to a sympathetic architect in the Piccadilly Arcade, close to Simpson. He showed his own products there, but also exhibited the work of other designers to attract an audience, and for a while started a secondary business importing basketware from Madeira with the writer Wolf Mankowitz. He bought a second-hand Vespa scooter, which propelled him across London between his various premises, customers and suppliers.

He quickly added a design studio to his original business of manufacturing furniture and fitting out interiors. The idea of the studio came from Ian Bradbery, a graphic designer whom Terence had met at the Central School. He asked Terence to make the exhibition displays, and Bradbery supplied the graphics.

Terence's own designs for his furniture company

The company was importing and distributing Italian furniture alongside its own production

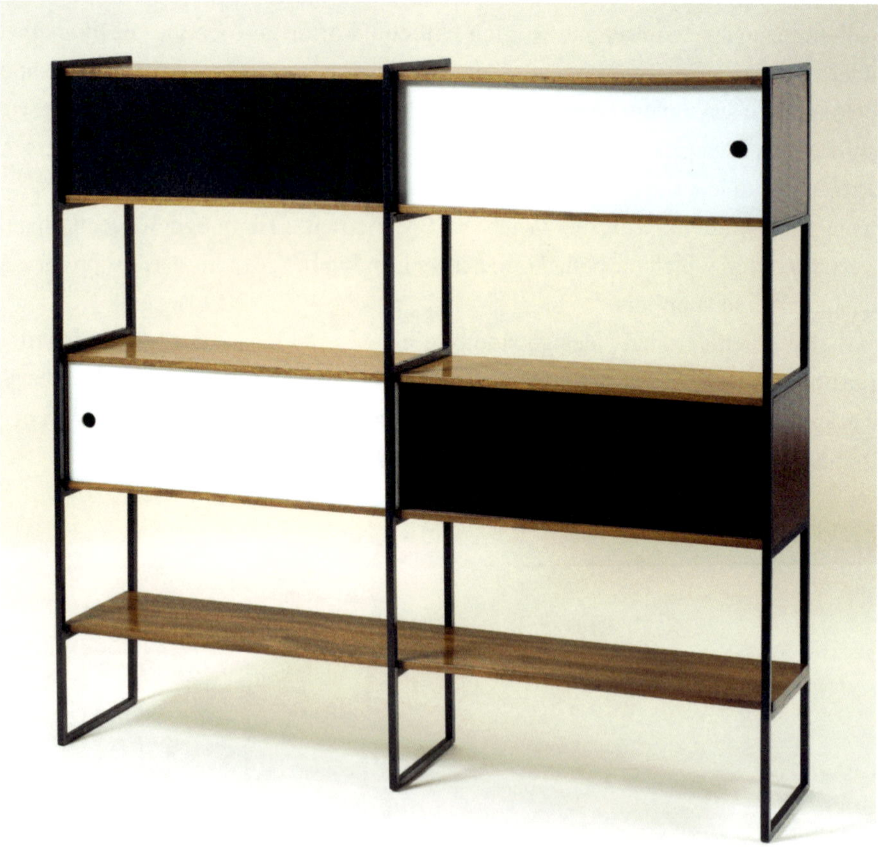

WORKING FOR HIMSELF

The basis for the Conran storage system was a welded steel frame. It also came with laminate and veneer finishes

Before the Second World War, most designers in Britain had worked as individuals, like Terence's teachers at the Central School, supplying manufacturers with sketches, drawings and plans, or a finished artwork. They were able to practise almost entirely on their own with a minimum of overheads and administration.

The early projects that Terence worked on – for Whitehead in textiles, Midwinter in ceramics and Wallpaper Manufacturers Ltd (WPM) for wallpaper – were all of this nature, and did not require him to build up a substantial organisation.

Terence was selling several designs in this way in the early 1950s. He worked on textile designs for Gerald Holtom, producing a scratchy linear pattern in 1951 that he called Totem. Holtom was a notable artist and designer himself, and produced the original version of the Campaign for Nuclear Disarmament symbol in 1958,

Pattern designed by Terence in 1949 when he was still a student

Chequers, a textile design by Terence from 1951

before Ken Garland simplified it. Terence also worked for A & F Parkes and Co. during this period; his key-pattern woven textile for the company dates to 1955.

Terence's work for Roy Midwinter at the Midwinter ceramics company followed a similar pattern to his relationship with David Whitehead & Sons Ltd. They were both long-established, family-owned businesses, and both were going through a period of modernisation. William Robinson Midwinter had been founded in 1910 in Burslem in Stoke-on-Trent. The company was doing well in the 1930s with its popular line of figurines, including Larry the Lamb and Peggy the Calf.

By 1951, a wave of consolidations had made it one of the largest employers in the Potteries, with more than 600 people.

Midwinter went to America in 1952 to look at how the ceramics industry was changing there and came back with a strategy for modernisation that involved investing in new families of products, and finding new ways of decorating them. Midwinter contacted Terence at his Piccadilly Arcade showroom and commissioned decorative designs from him. To capitalise on its investment, Midwinter immediately began to emphasise its designers in its marketing material.

The Nature Study series, for example, was advertised as having been designed by Terence Conran, and claimed it represented 'a genuine hand engraving, with permanent acid-resisting, underglaze colours', while its form was an example of Stylecraft fashion tableware by Midwinter.

Each piece of the Salad Ware range was stamped with the message 'Hand decorated in permanent underglaze colours, designed by Terence Conran'. Midwinter advertised Plant Life, a motif based on Terence's own designs for a planter in *House and Garden*. Less to Terence's taste would have been Midwinter's more popular advertising campaign from 1956, featuring Belinda Lee, a sultry-looking film star signed to the Rank Organisation, headlined 'Stylecraft, Fashion Tableware: a Midwinter Compliment to Beauty'.

Lee, who was soon to be seen in two Ealing Studio productions – *The Feminine Touch* and *Who Done It?* – is pictured floating above a selection of Midwinter products. The caption describes the tableware illustrated as being

> *from the new Stylecraft Fashion range, designed by Roy Midwinter. The pattern is Nature Study by Terence Conran, one of Britain's leading designers. The smooth black satin finish of the holloware contrasts delightfully with the modern design on the plates, saucers and lids.*

Terence's designs were sold alongside pieces with Hugh Casson's drawings and Peter Scott's wild geese.

Terence's relationship with Midwinter became more business-like. The following year Terence redesigned the company showroom in Stoke-on-Trent, and Midwinter took the Chequers pattern Terence had sold to David Whitehead and applied it to its ceramics.

'Roy seemed to be waging single-handed warfare in the Potteries of the mid 1950s, mark you, I also felt that I was in a trench myself in a grey depressed London, so it must have been even tougher in Stoke,' Terence wrote afterwards.[1] However, he made no secret of the fact that he would have preferred to be involved

TERENCE CONRAN   MAKING MODERN BRITAIN

WORKING FOR HIMSELF

The relationship with David Whitehead, the Lancashire textile firm, began when Terence was still at the Central School. The long established company was modernising itself by commissioning work from a new generation of designers. This piece, intended for use as a furniture fabric, was designed in 1952

TERENCE CONRAN   MAKING MODERN BRITAIN

WORKING FOR HIMSELF

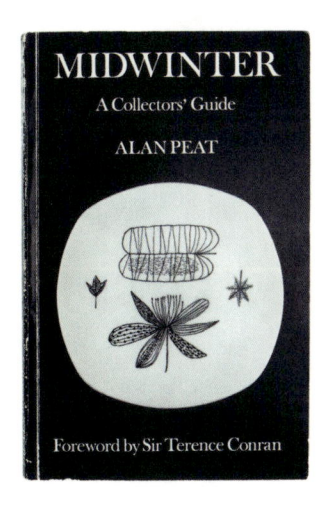

The Midwinter ceramics firm developed a strategy similar to that of Whitehead. Roy Midwinter asked Hugh Casson, Peter Scott and Terence to decorate his new products. Chequers, originally designed for use on textiles, appeared on one plate, and Terence sketched his own design for a planter on another

Midwinter's advertising campaign for its Fashion range put a film star's name first

For the professional market, the Conran name was highlighted

As well as working on individual products, Conran and Co. designed the Midwinter showroom in Stoke-on-Trent

TERENCE CONRAN   MAKING MODERN BRITAIN

with shaping Midwinter's products, rather than being confined to simply decorating existing pieces.

Terence introduced David Queensberry to Midwinter, which was to be the beginning of a long-term consultancy role. Midwinter remembered at that first meeting suggesting to Terence and Queensberry that 'the Potteries lived on the rose, the most abused flower God had invented. There must be a way to modernise the rose'. He also recalled that 'Terence began drawing; these things just flew out of his pen, like magic'.[2] Such commissions, which could be realised without an elaborate office infrastructure, gradually gave way to more complex projects that needed a studio with a sufficient range of skills to handle them.

The Modus wallpaper collection was a different proposition from the Whitehead textiles. In 1960, when Britain's Wallpaper Manufacturers Ltd (WPM), the holding company for the majority of the country's wallpaper brands, launched the Modus collection, Terence was a natural choice to contribute a number of wallpaper designs. It was part of a campaign to maintain the market for a product that was being challenged by the use of paint finishes and was exhibited at WPM's West End showroom. By this time Terence had a sizeable studio, and his name was important for Modus. He was also producing textiles on his own account, but Conran Fabrics was not limited to designs by Terence and Shirley Conran. For example, it commissioned several designs from Natalie Gibson such as Happy Dreams, a Day-Glo psychedelia-inspired screen-print that is now in the Victoria and Albert Museum's collection.

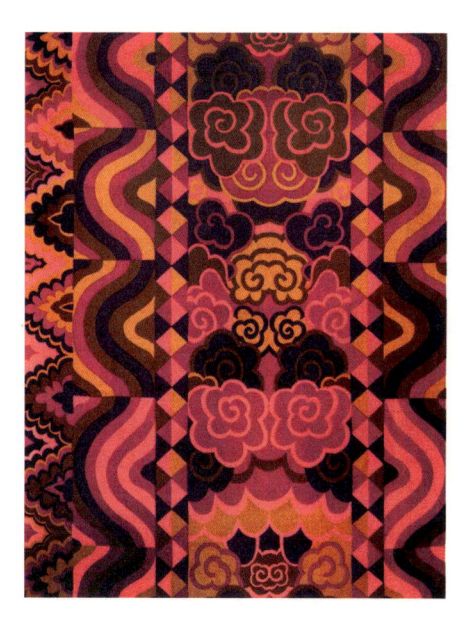

Conran Fabrics commissioned a wide range of textile designers, including Natalie Gibson for this piece

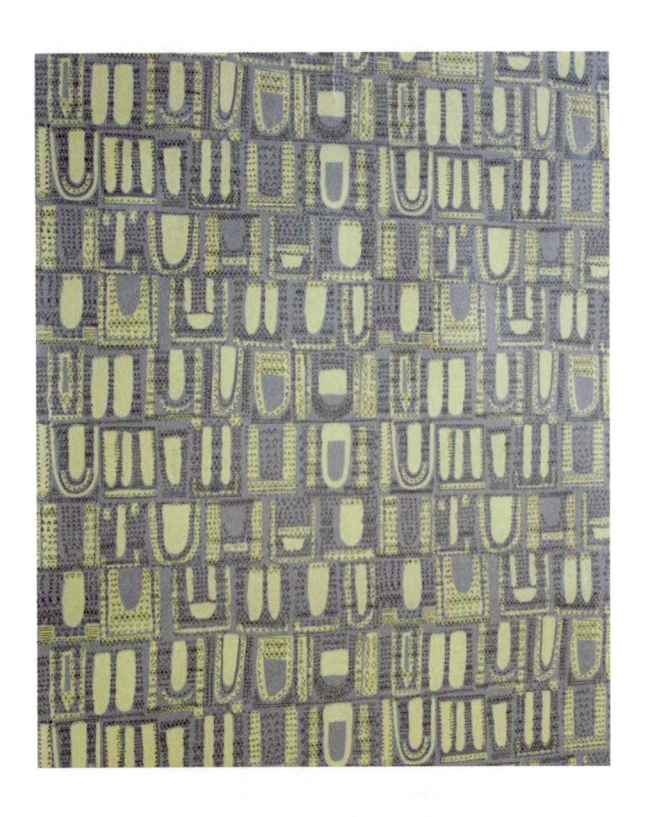

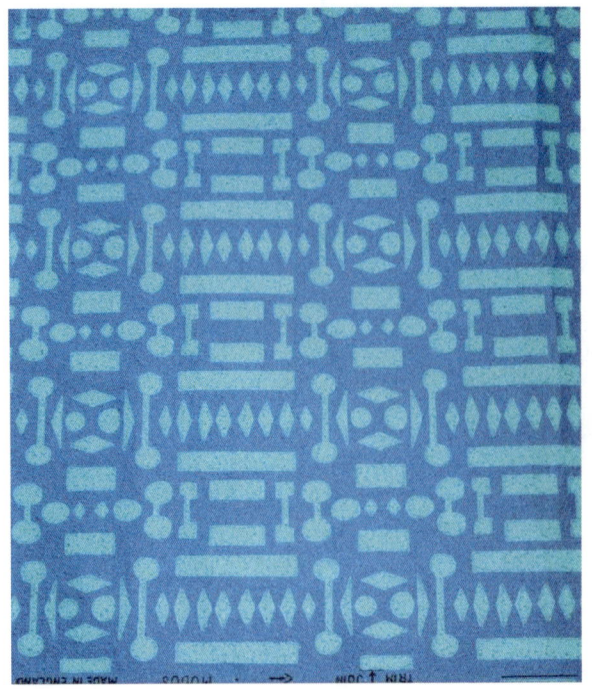

Portal M 1085, wallpaper designed in 1960 for the Modus Palladio collection, produced by Lightbown Aspinall (top). Cut Out (bottom) was from the same collection

British design practices were growing in scale and took on some of the structure adopted by the burgeoning advertising agencies, in which creatives had a somewhat different role from account managers and planners. An early model for the new design consultancies was the Design Research Unit (DRU), a name that seemed to have been deliberately chosen to suggest that it was a form of public service.

It was first established in 1943 by Marcus Brumwell, an impressively enlightened advertising executive, with the designers Milner Gray and Misha Black, and the writer Herbert Read. It set out to provide a range of services, from architecture to industrial design, with an unusual level of cultural ambition. In 1945, for example, when the DRU was working for the Jowett Motor Company for the design of a new car, it asked the sculptor Naum Gabo to work on a prototype. The DRU also designed displays for both the *Britain Can Make It* exhibition and the Festival of Britain.

As the economy opened up, the DRU designed showrooms for the Electricity Board, interiors for the P&O liner *Canberra* and, most famously, in the 1960s, the new corporate identity for Britain's railways. The heraldry that had defined the newly nationalised British Railways was abandoned in favour of the bold double arrow logo that survives to this day, and the new name British Rail (now National Rail).

The DRU was launched with a manifesto probably written by Herbert Read:

The machine is accepted as the essentially modern vehicle of form. Our designs will therefore be essentially designs for mass production, but at the same time we hope to rescue mass production from the ugliness and aesthetic emptiness which has so far characterised the greater part of its output. It is impossible to accept the view that any essential antagonism exists between art and industry, between beauty and the machine. But it is necessary to reintegrate the worlds of art and industry, for only on that basis can we progress to a new and vital civilisation.[3]

These were sentiments with which Terence would have agreed. As his business grew, he built a studio on a scale and with a sophistication that would match the range of work that DRU was taking on. Graphic designers and architects essentially belonged to different tribes, but the DRU showed how effective it could be when they worked together. Terence followed the same path. A contemporary consultancy, Pentagram, took another model based on individual partners retaining control of the business. This evolution of design consultancies continued in the 1980s when Rodney Fitch and Michael Peters built large-scale businesses that they were persuaded to float on the Stock Exchange, following the example of the advertising industry.

By 1955 Terence had moved his showroom from Piccadilly Arcade to Cadogan Lane, where he also based his design studio. He proudly advertised that he was selling his designs. These included his C4 chair, in a choice of basketweave or upholstery, and his low tables for the newly completed first terminal building at Heathrow. To demonstrate his own design capabilities, Terence used photographs of the executive dining room that he had designed for the razor blade company Gillette, equipped with his stacking chair from 1958, the C20. In the same advertisement, he also talked about installing pieces in the Hotel Leofric, part of the reconstruction of Coventry's town centre.

Ten years later, when Heathrow airport planned a large-scale expansion in 1968, Terence's involvement went far beyond supplying the seating. It was the Conran Design Group that was appointed to plan the interior of the new Terminal One, with Frederick Gibberd and Partners as architects. In a previous era, the architect would have had responsibility for both architecture and interior. But at Terminal One, planned for domestic and short-haul European flights, it was the Conran Design Group that designed the glass-fibre and chrome-steel check-in counters, the illuminated information graphics, the seating areas and the shops. In those days, before airports had been turned into giant out-of-town shopping malls in search of revenue, airport retailing was still decently restrained, rather than the obstacle course it has become today.

The C 20 stacking chair, designed in 1958, and manufactured in the Conran workshop in Fulham

With a design studio, as well as its own production facilities, Conran and Co. was able to specify its own products for commissions such as the interiors for the Gillette company

Terence had already broadened his repertoire to include shop design. Woolland Brothers, the department store in Knightsbridge whose furniture section turned out to be a good outlet for his products, commissioned him to create a new, more fashionable womenswear floor.

Terence would eventually set up Conran Roche, a full-blown architecture and planning consultancy, with Fred Lloyd Roche. Terence was asked to design offices for a rising generation of business meteors, including Michael Heseltine and the Saatchi brothers. But it wasn't only Terence's design studio that was growing. Over the course of ten years, Terence moved his workshops five times, beginning in the basement of the theatre in Notting Hill, moving to Donne Place in Chelsea, and then to the North End Road in Fulham before finding Cock Yard, a former jam factory in Camberwell. His final move in this period of his life was to leave London altogether in 1963 to set up in a new purpose-built factory in Thetford.

Each new location brought new individuals into the Conran orbit. In Notting Hill, it was O'Leary. In 1955 in Piccadilly Arcade, it was John Stephenson as a salesman, who later helped set up the Conran Design Group – and married Shirley Conran after her divorce from Terence. At Hanway Place, where the studio moved after Cadogan Lane, it was the designer Rodney Fitch, who joined him in 1961.

Terence's first restaurants were a key part of the work of his studio. They were a calling card, and a place to make connections. The publicity around the opening of the Soup Kitchen in 1953 created something of an aura around Terence. It was a place that attracted the kind of people who were starting out on their own careers. Mary Quant and Alexander Plunket Greene were seen there a lot, and Bernard and Laura Ashley were also regulars.

Terence did a lot of socialising with both the Quants and the Ashleys, and the growth of their three respective businesses followed similar lines. Plunket Greene

Rodney Fitch was a leading member of the Conran Design Group who went on to start his own consultancy

The design group shared a space in Hanway Place with the Conran showroom

opened the first Bazaar in the King's Road in 1955, after meeting Quant when they were both art students at Goldsmiths College. Initially Quant was the buyer, but she soon emerged as a very talented designer in her own right.

The second Bazaar opened in 1961 after a series of dinners with Terence in Alexander's, the restaurant in the basement of the King's Road Bazaar. Terence designed a site for the second Bazaar shop on Knightsbridge Green. It had a double-height space with a slick theatrical facade and bold graphics. And it was enough of an event when it opened that Leyland, the ailing giant of the British car industry, used the store as the backdrop for one of its advertising campaigns.

Triumph built one of the more successful post-war British cars, the Herald, styled by an Italian, Giovanni Michelotti. The advertisement appeared in *Vogue* magazine and featured an all-white convertible version of the car, parked outside Bazaar, with a young woman dressed head-to-foot in Quant, loaded with shopping bags. The message was: 'The girl gets dated. The Triumph Herald doesn't.'

Three years later Quant played a part in launching Habitat by dressing the shop staff in her clothes. By this time Terence was taking on larger commissions that needed a fair-sized team. The overall design process could no longer be the work of Terence alone, and he needed both the management skills of Stephenson to ensure that projects were well run, and a studio of designers to deliver them. By 1961 there were more than a dozen, including the young Fitch, working in Hanway Place alongside the textile and furniture showrooms.

WORKING FOR HIMSELF

Open favourite with youth, the Triumph Herald convertible

The girl gets dated. The Triumph Herald doesn't.

The design of the Triumph Herald was finalised when Eden was Prime Minister.

Two years later, in 1959, the car was launched. It was a sensation. It was the first British light car with all-independent suspension. The 25-ft turning circle gave new meaning to 'mobility'. The Herald also pioneered long-interval servicing, the multi-position driving seat, an all-round view for the driver, and the outsize boot.

Eight years later, people are still buying the Herald because it is the most up-to-the-minute car on the market. Some of the Herald's good points have been copied by other cars, but nothing has come along to make the Herald seem dated. And the Herald itself has got *better*. The engine has grown from 948 cc to 1147 cc. The chassis is now even stronger. The seats are deeper and more sumptuous.

The road to perfection

The Herald left any teething problems behind years ago. It is as near 'bugless' as a car can be. Because the development costs were recovered years ago, money has been available to improve the Herald's quality.

The Herald is a very successful paradox. It is an utterly contemporary motor with an 8-year record of progressive improvement.

Why people buy the Herald

Some people choose the Herald because they like innovation, and some people because they like known quantities. (And some people, such as the girl in the picture, choose the Herald convertible. It is the only really modern low-price 4-seat open car on the market today.) Why not put the Herald to the test on either count? Any Triumph dealer will not merely give you a test run in a Herald. He will let you drive it.

Triumph Herald 1200 £627.7.3
Convertible £691.5.7 · Estate £711.11.3
12/50 £677.15.2

TRIUMPH

Standard-Triumph Sales Ltd., Berkeley Square,
London W1 · Telephone GROsvenor 8060

An advertising campaign that relied on the reflected glamour of the Quant name and her new shop

Creating a comprehensive corporate identity for the Harveys drinks business was one of the Conran Design Group's largest projects, and combined graphics with interiors

That same year, the Harveys of Bristol commission was the most elaborate project taken on by the Conran Design Group to date. It took three years and involved every aspect of the wine importer's identity. It gave the company a new brand marque. It redesigned the characteristic Harveys sherry bottle together with its labels, delivery vehicles and off-licences. It also created a restaurant in the cellar of the Harveys headquarters in Bristol, where white-painted bare-brick walls and tiled floors, set off by an antique ship's figurehead from an old boat, prefigured the look of the first Habitat. The studio had a dozen designers or more, including Fitch and Oliver Gregory, but it was Terence's style that set the tone for all of them.

The different types of coverage Terence received in the *Architectural Review* and *House and Garden* – the first for a professional audience who might be expected to buy Terence's furniture for their clients, the second for the public who would be buying for their own living rooms – defined the two very different markets that would shape much of his future career. Terence built a factory in Thetford to supply the professionals and opened Habitat to cater for the public.

The problem for Terence was that it was much more difficult to make money from Habitat, and remain a purist about design, than it was to create a successful business out of the contract market. It also required a lot more working capital. But Terence had missionary zeal. He wanted to talk directly to a wide public. He preferred the platform it gave him to the safer but less visible contract market. He knew that there was a better way to do things, and he was always convinced that if only it was presented properly, the public would see it too.

This contradiction about the public versus trade markets was painfully exposed in the merger that Terence entered into with Ryman that saw Habitat, the Thetford factory and the Conran Design Studio become part of the office equipment business. The two Ryman brothers, who had the controlling stake in the combined business, dismissed the value of Habitat but could see the profitability of the contract market, and suggested in public that the primary attraction for the merger was the design group, whose tangible assets were its forty designers. The merger broke up within eighteen months.

In the long run, however, Terence had a shrewder understanding of the value of strong public recognition of the Conran name. Underneath all this activity, the broad outline of this stage of Terence's career was to run a design studio that both served his own business and worked for outside clients, and to make a variety of products himself during the decade in a series of buildings from a workshop in the basement of a theatre in Notting Hill to a modern purpose-built factory in Thetford, employing eighty people. He could use this furniture in Conran Design Group interior projects, thereby improving his profit either by cutting out the margin that other suppliers would take or by selling it to others.

Terence looked for all the markets for his products that he could find. The big advantage of selling to specifiers was that it was much less of a financial risk and required less up-front investment. He needed a showroom to make the most of the products he was offering to the contract market. This investment was limited to the display of his products, because he wouldn't put them into production until he had a firm order in place, and the contract orders were bigger than domestic furniture retailers could offer. An architect designing a university hall of residence

Part of the Harveys project involved the creation of a substantial restaurant in Bristol. Its repertoire of white painted brick walls set the style for the look of the Habitat stores

Conran and Co. moved its production facilities to a purpose-built factory in Thetford in 1963

After the short-lived merger of Conran with Ryman ended, the furniture factory remained with Ryman

or the interiors of a fleet of airliners was a much better prospect than doing business with a dozen different retailers. There was also money to be made from importing and marketing the products of other manufacturers. Terence's travels to Italy and Scandinavia in the 1950s had produced useful connections. He also found Italian suppliers for furniture such as Vico Magistretti's chairs and Kartell's plastic storage units. In the 1960s he was doing the same in India, and Habitat began selling dhurries, dyed to Terence's specifications. Conran Contracts by this time was already the UK agent for Marimekko, and for Jack Lenor Larsen textiles.

In the ten years from 1954 to 1964, when Terence opened the first Habitat, he was building up his capacity as a manufacturer step by step. He wanted to be like Hille, perhaps the most successful modern furniture manufacturer in Britain at the time, who sold Robin Day's polyprop chair in multiple millions, and had

A properly equipped modern factory, and a newly designed range of flat-pack furniture, gave Conran extra capacity which Habitat was meant to absorb

the licence to manufacture Mies van der Rohe's and Florence Knoll's designs for the British market.

Astonishingly, in the 1960s both local and national government believed that London, already down to a population of 7.5 million from its 1938 peak of 8.5 million, was overcrowded; the state was prepared to expend a great deal of money and effort to persuade a substantial proportion of these residents to leave. A ring of New Towns was built around London to house them, starting with Basildon and Harlow, and ending with Milton Keynes. Alongside this was a plan to expand existing towns, where local authorities collaborated with the London County Council to build new factories for firms that were being persuaded to leave the capital, and social housing for their workers. As a direct result, East London's once-thriving furniture industry disappeared as companies moved out, with printing following

The Summa range, created by the Conran Design Group, was intended to provide a complete selection of domestic furniture

close behind. Hille moved its factory to Haverhill in Suffolk. Terence was presented with three options by the London County Council and in 1961 it agreed to build his Thetford factory in Norfolk, in which he competed with Hille. Terence bought a house nearby in Dalham, where he spent long weekends.

The move gave him an impressive, modern factory designed in cream-coloured, fair-face brickwork by the LCC architects' department. Terence and the Conran Design Group designed the Summa flat-pack range specifically to be made in Thetford. Using ash wood, it included tables, beds, shelving and cupboards. But the business still needed a showroom in London if it was going to find a market for its products. And as he had done before, Terence combined his showrooms with a studio for his designers in 1961, moving from Cadogan Lane to Hanway Place.

[1] Alan Peat, *Midwinter: A Collector's Guide* (Dumfries and Galloway: Cameron & Hollis, 1992).
[2] Ibid.
[3] Michelle Cotton, *Design Research Unit 1942-72* (New York: Koenig Books, 2011), 1.

You are what you eat

TERENCE CONRAN MAKING MODERN BRITAIN

The memories of the generation that experienced a wartime childhood, as Terence did, were inevitably shaped by shortages. There wasn't much to eat, and what there was, was far from delicious. Germany's strategy at the start of the Second World War was to use its submarines to try to starve Britain by sinking the ships that brought in the food its fifty million people relied on. The ration book – which offered each adult the guarantee of just one fresh egg each week, along with an additional allowance of dried egg powder, four ounces of bacon and two ounces of butter – was the country's most effective defence. As a strategy, it worked. To reassure the government at the start of the war, the Ministry of Food carried out calorie-counting experiments, which suggested that even with worst-case shipping losses Britain could still feed itself enough to carry on the war. But it was not food as we know it. For a decade, there were no lemons or bananas to be had, and the supply of oranges was limited to pregnant mothers and young children. As the war went on, sausages depended more and more on bread for their bulk. The taste of fish and chips was tainted by the declining quality of the fats in which they were fried. Canned snoek, the fish imported from South Africa, turned out to be an unpopular substitute for cod.

The end of the war made little difference, and meat rationing continued until July 1954. The manufacture of staples such as bread, cheese and butter was controlled by the Ministry of Food and rationalised. It was a move that served to eliminate every variety of cheese except 'utility' cheddar and coarsened the quality of bread. But these measures did mean that there was enough to go round.

If they got hungry, the masses had the chance to stretch their rations by eating at one of the British Restaurants set up by the Ministry of Food throughout the country. These were communal kitchens staffed by volunteers in the green uniforms of the Women's Voluntary Service, offering cheap and filling, if unappetising, meals. From May 1943 onwards the elite, who had been able to skip the shortages by paying over the odds to eat in private restaurants, were also brought into line. A government decree restricted restaurant meals to no more than three courses, with meat limited to just one of them. The price was a maximum of five shillings per person, and a special licence was required to serve food after 11p.m.

Elizabeth David's evocative writing, initially for magazines and newspapers, later in a series of influential books, opened a generation of British consumers to the pleasures of fresh ingredients and imaginative cooking. She shaped the thinking of professional chefs as well as amateur cooks

The British cookery writer Elizabeth David returned to London after spending the war in Greece and Egypt, and was confronted by the unappetising prospect of life on a diet based on what she described as 'flour and water soup, seasoned solely with pepper; bread and gristle rissoles; dehydrated onions and carrots and corned beef toad in the hole'.[1] Her respite from this purgatory was, as she put it, to dream of lemons. This was a period when Lyons' Corner Houses served tinned spaghetti on toast. Terence remembered always feeling hungry, and never forgot the inadequacy of the Spam sandwiches he ate with Eduardo Paolozzi as a student.

Paradoxically, the general health of the country improved substantially, even as the general dissatisfaction with the diet, imposed by the government, grew. Infant mortality fell and life expectancy, excluding deaths from enemy action, rose thanks to low-fat and low-sugar balanced diets with adequate vitamins.

As soon as the restrictions on restaurants were lifted in 1950, this picture began to change. Despite the poor ingredients available, the restricted skills of cooks, and a general English suspicion of the Continental staples of olive oil and garlic, enthusiastic amateurs began to open a wave of new restaurants in London. To encourage the newcomers, and to campaign against what he called 'cruelty to food', Raymond Postgate published the first edition of the *Good Food Guide* in 1951. It was a democratic introduction to eating out. The Ox on the Roof, named in tribute to the famous Parisian artist's cabaret patronised by Josephine Baker and Francis Picabia, opened that year at 353 King's Road in Chelsea. The London namesake, which offered snails, grilled scampi and a mixed grill, was run by an émigré Slav called Albert, and his British wife Ruby. Eating there was a highlight of Terence's social life for a time. He fondly remembered eating the entrecôte, ratatouille and strawberry tart, with a carafe of wine.

After Terence sold his share in the Soup Kitchen in 1954, he spotted that the property next door to the Ox was for rent. He decided to take the lease and open a restaurant of his own, which he named the Orrery.

Terence also used to eat at Le Matelot, which was opened on Elizabeth Street in Belgravia in 1952 by one of the more exotic restaurant enthusiasts of the period, Dr Hilary James. There was talk of Terence designing a second restaurant for James in Brighton. According to Fanny and Johnnie Cradock's review of Le Matelot:

> *You will either be enchanted by this small restaurant or embarrassed. It is unique. The proprietor, Dr. Hilary James, is a psychiatrist by day and a restaurateur by night.*
>
> *On Christmas Eve he wears horns. We keep a regular date there on Christmas Eve now. The staff are young, gay, inconsequential and yet highly efficient and courteous. But Le Matelot is informal. Witness, the extremely pretty young Miss who, on our first visit, plonked our ratatouille down on the table, remarking casually, 'mon Dieu, quel Plonk'. This same nymph, wearing coral jeans, exposed midriff, holly in her fair curls and mistletoe in her buttonhole, nonchalantly removed a champagne cork, poured the wine (not for us – we dislike drinking champagne all through a meal) and tossed the cork back down the restaurant to a colleague in a South American hat, a printed silk blouse and a pair of somewhat startling pants. 'Corky,' he said – quite untruthfully – as he smelled the cork. Then both grinned at the contented customer and continued to carry in dishes of Avocado Vinaigrette (3s.), Coquilles St Jacques (3s.), Corn on the Cob (2s. 6d.), New England Grilled Gammon with Sweetcorn (6s.), Poulet Henry IV (5s.), superb Stilton cheese (2s. 6d.), and Dames Blanches (2s.) for the sweet-toothed.*
>
> *It is a delightfully uninhibited, scatty little place, brimming with custom, canopied with fish-nets, discreetly lit and gay, gay, gay, in our stuffed shirt old town.*[2]

Le Matelot was run for Dr James by Bruce Copp, a theatre-world restaurateur, a favourite of Judi Dench and a close friend of Hattie Jacques. Copp eventually quit Le Matelot, exasperated at his employer's casual habit of recruiting unskilled young men from the streets of Piccadilly and offering them jobs in the kitchen.

The Soup Kitchen, which opened in 1953 on Chandos Place, close to Charing Cross, was Terence's first venture into restaurants on his own account. It had been planned with Ivan Storey at the kitchen table in their house in Warwick Gardens, and was designed to offer appetising food without the expense of employing a professional chef. It was based on what Conran had picked up from six weeks spent in Paris working in the kitchens of La Méditerranée. This was a classic restaurant in Place de l'Odéon, with carpets on the floor, a menu designed by Jean Cocteau, murals painted by Marcel Vertès and Christian Bérard in the high-ceilinged dining room, and fish soup a speciality. He was living in some style in an apartment on the rue Jacob rented by an affluent American girlfriend, Betsy Scherman. She would later marry the artist Richard Smith. Terence loved Paris, but with little command of French he had a tough time washing up in the brutish conditions of an airless restaurant kitchen, where he watched one member of kitchen staff smuggling a side

Terence spent six weeks working as a washer-up in Paris in the kitchens at La Méditerranée, learning how to make soup, rather than in the magnificent dining room with its murals

of beef out of the meat safe and through the door to the street tucked into the front of his trousers. However, he learned enough from what he saw to understand how to make the stock that was going to be at the heart of his café. It taught him how to clarify stock with eggshells, and how to set up four smaller pots in bains-marie, always one for split peas, and one for minestrone, and others that might be vichyssoise or onion to flavour different versions of the product. Terence had devised what was in essence a fast-food restaurant.

He found suppliers for fresh-baked baguettes and apple flan, and offered cheddar cheese. There was no alcohol on the menu, but he did serve coffee. Terence and Storey drove to Turin to collect a second-hand Gaggia to make espresso, and then struggled to find somebody who knew how to plumb it in. The soup was sold by the pint in blue-and-white striped mugs.

YOU ARE WHAT YOU EAT

Chairs, tables, storage and textile print all designed by Terence in his showroom, lined, like his restaurants, in tongue and groove board

Newspaper coverage of the first Soup Kitchen, which opened in London on Chandos Place

Terence on his trip to France with Michael Wickham. Drawing by Patricia Lyttelton

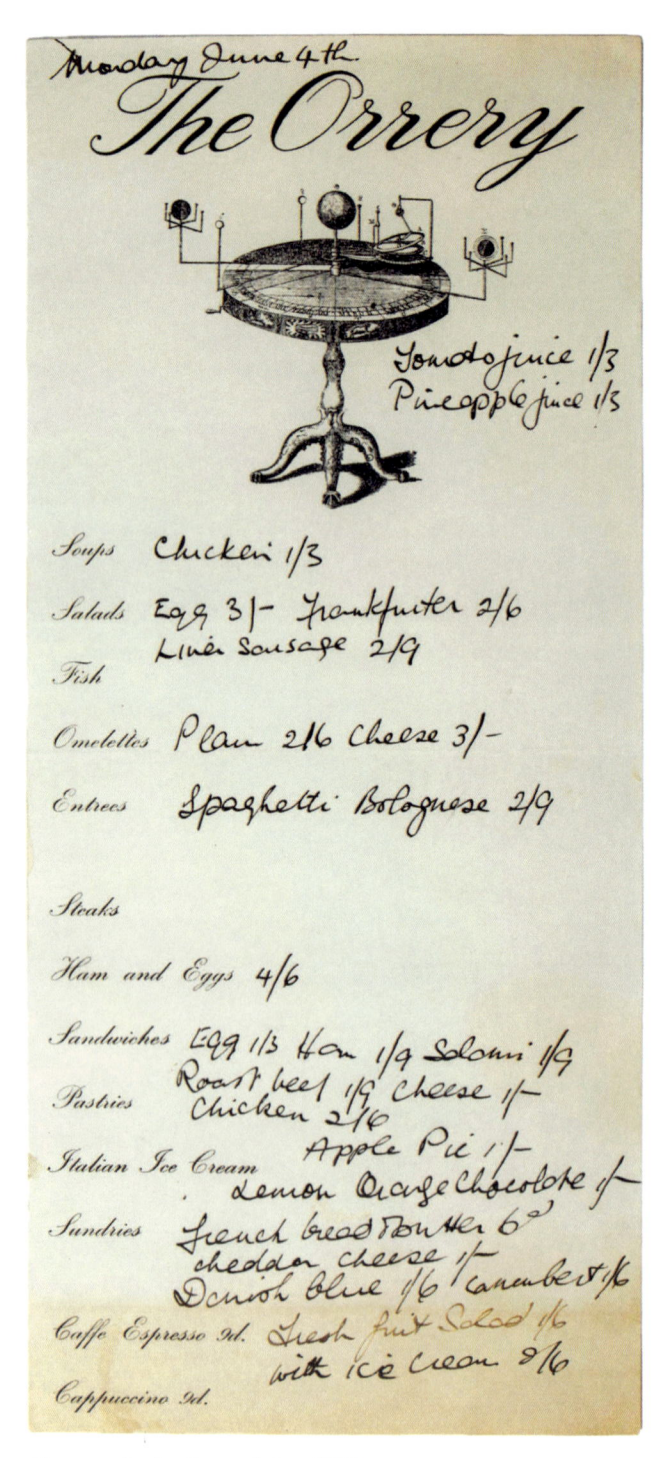

The menu for the Orrery, 4 June 1954

YOU ARE WHAT YOU EAT

It was called a coffee bar, but the Orrery offered more elaborately prepared food than the Soup Kitchen

The interior of the Orrery was finished with tongue and groove board

Terence designed the interior, which had chequered quarry-tiled floors, tongue-and-groove boarded walls, a slate-topped counter and photographic enlargements of Victorian engravings of vegetables on the walls. He also made the furniture, setting out the strategy that would continue to underpin his approach until the end of his life, when Benchmark was making the fittings that Conran and Partners designed for the restaurants that Conran owned and operated.

From the beginning, Terence was an adroit publicist. He offered a free meal to a group of homeless men, to allow the *Evening News* the chance to run a diary story about the irony of some smart young things opening a café named the Soup Kitchen and getting flooded with genuine tramps. He also got word to the cast of the newly opened production of *Guys and Dolls* that this would be a smart place to relax post-performance at the London Colosseum, just up the street on St Martin's Lane.

The Soup Kitchen was a hit. Terence ran the café during the day, and Ivan Storey came in to take over in the evenings after finishing his hospital rounds. They quickly set out to capitalise on their early success by opening three more Soup Kitchens: one in Cambridge; one on Shoe Lane, around the corner from what was then the Daily Express Building on Fleet Street, where Terence installed a row of telephones along the wall in the hope that journalists would be using them to dictate copy back to their offices; and another on Wilton Crescent in Belgravia.

The publicity for the Soup Kitchens attracted new clients for Terence who were looking for some of the glamour that he had brought to restaurant design. Walter Baxter, a novelist with independent means (who was prosecuted, but acquitted, for obscenity after the *Sunday Express* denounced him to its five million readers for *The Image and the Search*, a book it claimed was encouraging guiltless promiscuity), commissioned Terence to design a restaurant for him, the Chanterelle, which opened on the Old Brompton Road in 1953. It occupied the whole of a red-brick building that is now occupied by a Japanese restaurant, Yashin Ocean Sushi. The American food critic Colman Andrews, who didn't get there until the 1970s, described it as 'the first really good London English as opposed to Indian, French or suchlike restaurant that I ever dined in'.[3] Its specialities included one dish of brown beans, dates, onions and anchovies, as well as scallops in sea-urchin sauce. Elizabeth David became a regular. The veteran food writer Robin McDouall remembered it as a 'cosy, woody bistro in a free-standing brick building with cathedral windows. Terence Conran did the decor, with his inimitable lack of decorator's chi-chi'.[4]

Terence used natural wood finishes as he had done at the Soup Kitchen. Taking his cue from the ICA's *Parallel of Art and Nature* exhibition, he suspended flat panels from the ceiling at a variety of angles, in this case carrying engravings of

The success of the Soup Kitchen brought in the commission to design the Chanterelle

mushrooms from botanical textbooks. At the opening, Vivien Leigh complained about the lighting, saying it was unflattering. The inside faces of the shades hanging over the tables were subsequently painted pink.

Meanwhile, Terence and Ivan Storey had diverged in their views on how to run the business. Storey bought Terence out, and he took the money and used it to open a more elaborate restaurant on the King's Road, in a terraced house at the World's End long-since demolished. The Orrery had a longer menu, a proper chef and – unusual for its time – a garden, in which Terence built a barbecue. Over the course of an unusually long and warm summer it was a big attraction. Terence kept an Orrery menu, dated 4 June 1954, until the end of his life. It was a pre-printed form, categorised into soups, salads, fish, omelettes, sandwiches and entrées. The dishes of the day were handwritten. Even though it was called a coffee bar in a sign above the entrance, it featured substantial food: steaks, ham and eggs, salami sandwiches, and Frankfurter salad.

It was a long way from the menu at the second Orrery restaurant that Terence opened on Marylebone High Street in 1997. By this time, restaurants were at the heart of Terence's business rather than being an enthusiastic sideline. He was encouraged by the Howard de Walden Estate, in their plans to revitalise Marylebone High Street, to take on a handsome former stable building, open a branch of the Conran Shop at street level and use the upper floor as a restaurant. Within three years Chris Galvin, the chef, had won a Michelin star, the first for the Conran Group.

For the first Orrery, Terence designed an interior that was more elaborate than those he had done for the Soup Kitchen. But, as at the Chanterelle, there were photographic blow-ups on the walls, and a series of flat panels suspended

The Orrery's interior, with Terence's furniture, and blown-up enlargements of Victorian engravings from the ceiling to disrupt the spatial qualities of the main room, in the manner of Richard Hamilton's exhibition at the ICA that Terence had seen earlier in the year. It was a concept that Hamilton himself had borrowed from a study made by the Austrian graphic designer Herbert Bayer when he was at the Bauhaus. Terence used a sequence of food photographs taken by his sister Priscilla, then a student at Guildford School of Art, to create a striking window display.

And it was at the Orrery that Terence first met his second wife Shirley Pearce, while she was still an art student. At the time she was in a relationship with the potter David, Marquess of Queensberry. The two were walking from the Chelsea School of Art, based in Manresa Road on a turning off the King's Road, and trying

Shirley Conran in the house on Regent's Park Terrace, with the Orrery, a model of the solar system, after which the restaurant was named

to get a table next door at the Ox on the Roof. It was full, so they stood outside the window of the Orrery to wait. Peering in through the window, Shirley recognised one of Terence's chairs from a picture she had seen in an issue of the *Architectural Review*. Terence came to the door and asked them in for a closer look. She went back later for a meal.

In the early days of their relationship, Terence would walk past Simpson with Shirley after going out for dinner in the West End, admiring its glamorous modernist facade and its travertine-lined interior. He would talk to her about how it was the place that he would one day love to own.

Terence had already bought his first home, an early Victorian house built in 1840 on Regent's Park Terrace, a handsome street not actually in the park, but cut

Mark Boxer's cartoon strip 'Life and Times in NW1' satirised the Stringalongs, Terence's neighbours in Regent's Park Terrace

off from the Outer Circle by the main railway line into Euston, and close to the men's hostel on Arlington Road in which George Orwell spent some time while researching for his book *Down and Out in Paris and London*. It is where Shirley and Terence began their married life in 1955, at a time when life in two streets in the NW1 postcode, Regent's Park Terrace and Gloucester Crescent, had not yet been satirised by Alan Bennett and Mark Boxer. The terrace is the straight string to the curved bow of the crescent, with the two divided by long, narrow gardens like medieval strip farming. The houses on the terrace were more sober than those on the elaborately ornate Gloucester Crescent which backs on to it, but the houses in both streets were part of a development that had failed to live up to the original promoter's dreams of extending the prestige of Nash's terraces in Regent's Park into the railway lands of Camden Town. At the start of the 1950s the area was decidedly down-at-heel: the houses had been subdivided and turned into lodging-houses that let out inexpensive rooms to Irish and Caribbean migrants.

The combination of the closeness of these houses to the lush green splendour of Regent's Park and Central London beyond it, and the rock-bottom prices that they could be bought for in 1950 made them irresistible to highly educated young married couples, working as journalists, publishers, architects and academics looking for a first home. Terence, with his eye for promising neighbourhoods, was one of the first to arrive. Stephen Frears, the film director, lived there while he was married to Mary-Kay Wilmers, founder of the *London Review of Books*, as well as the artist David Gentleman, the philosopher AJ Ayer, the academic Claus Moser, the actor, director and doctor Jonathan Miller, and the performer George Melly. This became a world whose members were prepared to mock and parody themselves. Mark Boxer's cartoon strip 'Life and Times in NW1' first appeared in *The Listener* magazine in 1966. It chronicled the brittle lives of Simon and Joanna Stringalong. Boxer, the first editor of *The Sunday Times* magazine, drew Simon in kipper ties, with sideburns straggling down each cheek. Joanna had severe glasses and a Vidal Sassoon bob. A Habitat-like furniture emporium made an appearance under the name 'Bivouac'. Their models, visually at least, were Gloucester Crescent residents Claire Tomalin, at one time the literary editor of *The Sunday Times* and later the biographer of Dickens and Pepys, and her first husband Nick Tomalin, the war reporter killed on the Golan Heights by a Syrian missile in 1973.

Boxer had taken the idea from a television satire created by Alan Bennett, another resident of Gloucester Crescent. According to Bennett:

Like me, the Stringalongs had taken up residence in Victorian Camden Town and, along with so many other buyers of the still relatively cheap ex-rooming houses, had 'knocked through' their basements to make a commodious kitchen-dining room, shoved the nanny in the attic and crammed the house with collectable items from the many junk stalls of the neighbourhood.[5]

Bennett could have been describing Terence's life at 11 Regent's Park Terrace with Shirley. Before their marriage Terence was paying the mortgage by letting out rooms in the house, including for a time to the poet Christopher Logue, whom he had encountered in Paris during his time washing dishes at La Méditerranée.

'Rather sooner in life than they had expected, and not altogether in accordance with their liberal principles, the Stringalongs found themselves property-owners,' wrote Bennett about the soul-searching of a group of newcomers, painfully aware that their home-making was having the effect of pushing out others.

We were genuinely uneasy about it – or there would have been no need for jokes; and though our unease could be handily recycled into resentment of those who bought into the area later than we had, there was a definite sense that we were shoving the indigenous population out. A nice instance of this came one evening in 1965 when a dinner party in one of our newly knocked-through kitchens was interrupted by an old man, not

Bentwood rocker, antiques and Terence's own storage system at Regent's Park Terrace

quite a tramp, who rang at the door asking for the landlady. The last time he had been in London he had rented a room in this house and was there one available now? It was hard to explain that things had changed and it was again bad conscience that made us put him in a car and tour round Camden Town looking for a rooming house that had retained its integrity and was still a going concern. Later I wrote a sketch based on the incident which we filmed for one of the Sherrin programmes, coarsening it in the process: the old man became quite definitely a tramp and my Mini a Rolls-Royce (partly, though, to accommodate the camera crew) and the social implications nowhere. Still, it was this that gave me the idea for 'Life and Times in NW1'.[6]

Shirley Conran remembers something similar happening in their house on Regent's Park Terrace. 'In summer we left the front door open, and I remember once coming down the stairs to find a middle-aged woman dressed all in pink, who gave me her suitcase and asked to rent a room.'[7]

Before their two sons were born, Terence and Shirley lived on the top floor, which Terence designed and furnished, and had a studio on the first floor. They used their home as a showcase for their work. They were photographed in it, as the starting point for the growing celebrity of both partners. The house itself was published as an example of contemporary interior design in *Queen* magazine, the magazine owned by Michael Heseltine. *House and Garden* featured Terence and Shirley's home in its pages with a Charles and Ray Eames wire chair, Gio Ponti's Superleggera chairs, which had only just gone into production, and Terence's own storage system in the kitchen. In one white-painted brick room was a world globe

Studio space at Regent's Park Terrace

TERENCE CONRAN

PRINTED TEXTILE DESIGN

THE STUDIO HOW TO DO IT SERIES · 74

TERENCE CONRAN   MAKING MODERN BRITAIN

YOU ARE WHAT YOU EAT

Terence published his first book in 1957. It's a practical guide for students that combines technical and business advice with ideas about aesthetic and creative inspiration, covering all forms of textile design from furniture to fashion. It includes interviews with artists, designers and manufacturers, and examples of contemporary textile design – including his own work. He designed the book himself

133

that had been a gift to Terence from his mother for his twenty-first birthday, and kilims on the floor.

It was here that Terence and Shirley produced their book *Printed Textile Design*, part of a How To Do It series published by The Studio, which also owned *Art & Industry* magazine. The series included Ansel Adams on making a photograph, Tom Eckersley on poster design and Milner Gray on packaging design.

The book itself was a concise and imaginative introduction to the subject; it was also a reflection of how Terence was seen by the design world at that time, and the way in which he was accumulating people who were useful, influential and gifted. They interviewed, among others, Bernard Ashley, the managing director of a textile and fashion business that was not yet called Laura Ashley; Zikmund (Zika) Ascher, whose Matisse project Terence had worked on; Alexander Girard, the famous American textile designer; Astrid Sampe, the Swedish textile designer whose work Terence had seen – and been inspired by – at the Milan Triennale in 1954, and Lucienne and Robin Day, the golden couple of British design. They also talked to Dr Hilary James, the flamboyant psychiatrist at St George's Hospital who had opened Le Matelot restaurant.

The book was peopled by Terence and Shirley's friends, allies and family. Priscilla Conran photographed a selection of Fornasetti designs and Peter Todd Mitchell's scarves for Bianchi Ferrini. Priscilla's employers at the time, Hans and Elsbeth Juda, owners of *The Ambassador* magazine, were photographed in their apartment in Palace Gate, the block in Kensington designed by their friend, Wells Coates, to whom they introduced Terence. Elsbeth had studied photography with Lucia Moholy-Nagy. Hans employed László Moholy-Nagy as an art director, and famously coined the slogan 'Export or Die'. The book shows some of Terence's own textile work, as well as that of Shirley Conran, as well as Ian Bradbery's design for a stand at the London Medical Exhibition in 1951. Bradbery and Terence would go on working together into the 1960s. Terence picked out Jacqueline Groag, who had been part of the Rayon Design Centre team, to show a cotton screen-print of hers made for Haworth Fabrics. Terence also showed Sir Francis Rose's textiles for Bianchi Ferrini, Dior and Balenciaga.

The book was written just as Conran Fabrics, set up in partnership with a Manchester mill owner, Charles Winer, was starting to become successful. Shirley's determined presentation to Hugh Casson secured an order from his firm to fit out the interior of the BEA fleet of Viscount airliners.

The book is a bracing mixture of shrewd practicality and poetic inspiration, and is clearly the work of both Shirley and Terence. It invites designers to consider their work from the point of view of the consumer.

A successful design, when displayed in a store window, attracts customers to that store. The customer is attracted to a fabric by the colour and the design. Men seldom buy textiles. A woman considers a dress material in relation to the rest of her wardrobe, and against her complexion: she visualises a furnishing fabric in her home, with her furniture and walls if she is looking for material for windows, with her other furniture and curtains if she is looking at an upholstery fabric. Then she looks at the price. If she still wants to buy it, she considers the strength of the material, especially if the fabric is intended for upholstery or for children. Lastly the cleaning possibilities are considered.[7]

Shirley, for these can only be her words, goes on to point out that:

Vivid colours do not always flatter a woman's complexion, or her measurements. It is erroneously supposed that quiet, pastel shades are most suitable for a bedroom scheme because they are peaceful and soothing. The fact that people wake up in bedrooms as well as go to sleep in them, should be considered.[8]

Elsewhere, the words, considerately pitched for insecure students, may be Shirley's, but they are clearly based on lessons hard-learned by Terence.

When a manufacturer refuses your work, ask him politely why he doesn't want to buy it and be prepared to discuss what he is looking for. Very often it isn't because he dislikes your appearance and thinks your work is terrible. Perhaps he doesn't want floral designs, but is looking for abstracts ... perhaps his firm is conservative, and your colours are too bright ... perhaps he's just not buying at this time of year ... Don't be too persistent, you may get injured. Always take a definite 'no' for an answer when it is given for the second time ...

Don't forget that the client is a businessman. If he makes you feel that your designs are terrible but doesn't actually tell you to take them out of his sight, he's interested all right ... Don't let the client make you feel that you ought to be paying him to accept your designs.

Never let your designs out of your sight while in a prospective buyer's office, and never, never leave your designs for 'a day or two for consideration'. It might be quite safe but, again, it might not.[9]

Michelin House was the UK headquarters for the French tyre company until 1985

The first floor of the Michelin House was transformed into the Bibendum restaurant. The ground floor became the Conran Shop, while new office floors were inserted into the centre of the structure

TERENCE CONRAN   MAKING MODERN BRITAIN

Apart from its practical good sense, the book also reflects on the place of textile design in the wider cultural landscape. It discusses inspiration that the Festival of Britain Pattern Group took from molecular structures; it highlights the delicate structures of early machines. And it concludes that 'never before has fabric design been so directly influenced by contemporary painting and sculpture'.[10]

The book gives a picture of a close and influential circle that reflected life in Regent's Park Terrace. Under the influence of Shirley's outgoing personality, the house became a place to invite people who were both interesting and possibly useful: Basil Spence, who by that time had won the competition to rebuild Coventry Cathedral, came for dinner, as did Elizabeth David. Shirley had begun work at the *Daily Mail* and commissioned David to write for the paper.

Sebastian and Jasper Conran were born in Regent's Park Terrace. Jasper and Shirley would both later buy houses on the same street, but it is also where Terence

The Blueprint Café, on the first floor of the Design Museum, overlooking the Thames and Tower Bridge, opened in 1989. It was the start of a restaurant cluster that would eventually include Le Pont de la Tour, Cantina del Ponte and the Chop House

and Shirley's marriage fell apart under the strain of two high-pressure careers and continual anxieties about money, as well as Terence's closeness to his assistant at the time, Christina Smith. Terence in the early days always financed his business out of the cash that it generated. That made him continually vulnerable, and he developed relationships with customers he could rely on to pay quickly. He knew for instance that Olivetti, if offered a five per cent discount, would pay on delivery. There were times when he would go around personally on the last Friday of the month to its Berkeley Square headquarters to collect Olivetti's cheque so that he could bank it immediately to pay his staff their wages.

By the time that NW1 had reached the peak of its fame, Terence and Shirley were getting divorced and Terence had moved out. Then, after his divorce settlement

Le Pont de la Tour, which opened in 1991, was the most ambitious of Terence's restaurants, with a £1.6-million investment

Within weeks of Tony Blair's first election victory in 1997, Bill and Hillary Clinton came to London on a state visit. Their dinner at Le Pont de la Tour was a well-publicised part of the trip

YOU ARE WHAT YOU EAT

Quaglino's had been a celebrated restaurant in the past, even attracting the Queen. In its new incarnation, Terence tried to recapture the glamour in an entirely newly reconstructed building

The new Quaglino's shared the same address as the original, but was a completely new building. The central staircase at the centre of the dining room allows patrons to make a grand entrance on their way to the tables. It survived a redesign by Russell Sage Studio in 2014

with Shirley, he briefly moved back to the terrace before setting up home in Fitzroy Square with Caroline Herbert, who would become his third wife. They later moved to a house in St Andrews Place, on the south side of Regent's Park. It had a scale far grander than Regent's Park Terrace, and a creamy stucco-fronted facade.

The Soup Kitchens and the Orrery were short-lived diversions that Terence sold on, and he used the money they generated to invest in what, at the time, were his central preoccupations: the design, manufacture and sale of furniture. The Neal Street Restaurant was different and represented longer-term enthusiasm. Bibendum, which was started when Terence and the publisher Paul Hamlyn bought the French tyre manufacturer's London base in 1987, took that to another level with Simon Hopkinson, the chef that Terence persuaded to join him from Hilaire.

It was only after his leaving Storehouse that restaurants became a key part of Terence's business, along with his architecture and design practice, retailing at the Conran Shop and manufacturing at Benchmark.

The Blueprint Café came first: located inside the Design Museum at Shad Thames on the south side of the River Thames. Terence had wanted to call it the River Café East, but Ruth Rogers and Rose Gray, founders of London's original River Café, persuaded him not to. Instead, he named it after *Blueprint* magazine, and hung a row of its covers along one wall next to his Paolozzi prints.

Butler's Wharf had gone into receivership, but Terence used the ground floor of the Victorian warehouses that stretched from the Design Museum to Tower Bridge, between the river and the canyon-like Shad Thames on the land side, to create a string of restaurants, one after the other, orientated towards the river, each with its own identity. There was also a food shop and a wine merchant. The most ambitious of the restaurants, Le Pont de la Tour, opened in 1991 with a £1.6-million investment. It was followed by Cantina del Ponte, and then the Chop House, offering respectively French, Italian and British dishes. The restaurants succeeded in attracting customers from the other side of the river and played a significant part in revitalising the area.

But it was only in 1993, when Terence reopened Quaglino's, a once-famous name, that he conclusively reshaped the British restaurant scene. With 400 seats, 15,000 square feet and an investment of £2.6 million, Quaglino's was a giant restaurant, and an industrial-scale business. It also created a new version of public life for London. An elaborate central staircase, which descended through the middle of the main space filled with mirrors and colour, was designed to allow diners to make a grand entrance.

Past the reception desk and the spot-lit vase of exotic flowers, you found yourself at the start of a sequence of cascading stairs, the first with a sinuous brass handrail, which curled around a Dhruva Mistry bas relief depiction of a woman and a monkey, before bringing you to the bar, a kind of promenade deck that looked out over the main restaurant below. The second, a sweeping flight of white marble steps that would not have disappointed Errol Flynn at his most swashbuckling, tumbled down into the bowels of the restaurant, a vast prairie of linen and wine glasses, that swept to the horizon, culminating in an elaborately mosaiced oyster bar. Quaglino's was the last Conran project that Keith Hobbs, who had worked with Terence since the Neal Street Restaurant, was involved with. At the start of the following year, he started his own studio.

Shortly after the opening of Quaglino's, Terence met Vicki Davis, whom he married in 2000. She started to work with him on the new restaurant openings that came with increasing speed as Terence started plates spinning across London – from Almeida in Islington to the Bluebird in Chelsea.

Conran made restaurants big enough to function as a species of street theatre and triggered a shortage of chefs and waiters in the process. So successful was the Conran approach to restaurants that, for a while, getting one suddenly became a must-have status symbol for ambitious provincial cities.

Just as the Soup Kitchen attracted clients looking for Terence to design their restaurants in the 1950s, the success of Quaglino's and Terence's redevelopment of the gone-to-seed Great Eastern Hotel at Liverpool Street Station did the same in the 1990s. Vicki worked on the Trieste hotel project in Vienna. And in Paris, Terence enjoyed opening the Alcazar in 1998 with a French partner, not far from La Méditerranée where he had his first restaurant job forty-five years earlier.

The same collecting impulse that drove Terence's pursuit of butterflies as a child, and gave him the chance to build up Storehouse, came into play with Terence's delight in opening new restaurants, and continually moving on to the next new project, sometimes at the cost of maintaining the sense of commitment of the staff left behind to carry out the daily routine of operating a big and complex restaurant.

Vicki Conran cautioned against overexpansion: in particular trying to run Guastavino's on the wrong site in New York, and opening a Conran Shop in the wrong part of Dublin. But for Terence, they were all irresistible challenges.

Terence's restaurants depended on a range of people for their success, chefs that included Galvin at the Orrery, Hopkinson at Bibendum, and Jeremy Lee at the Blueprint Café, and managers such as Joel Kissin, who opened Le Pont de la Tour, Quaglino's and Guastavino's under the Queensboro Bridge in New York. Design and art were always part of the mix. Richard Smith was commissioned to make an installation at the Bluebird on the King's Road. Allen Jones did a striking screen for Mezzo in Soho.

Des Gunewardena, recruited by Terence from Gerald Ronson's Heron Company to work as the finance director for Conran Roche, became the chief executive of the Conran restaurants that stretched across thirty-two sites in Britain, France, Sweden and America. He was as interested in expanding to more sites as Terence. In 2006, Gunewardena and David Loewi bought a forty-nine per cent stake in the restaurants for their company D&D. Bibendum was always a separate business from the Conran Restaurant group. It was owned equally by Terence, Paul Hamlyn and Simon Hopkinson. It is now owned by three of Terence's children, Michael Hamlyn and the current chef, Claude Bosi. Terence went on to open the Boundary and Lutyens. In 2012, Terence sold his remaining stake in D&D.

[1] Elizabeth David, *An Omelette and a Glass of Wine* (London: Grub Street, 1986).
[2] Bon Viveur, *Bon Viveur's London and the British Isles* (London: Dakers, 1955).
[3] Colman Andrews, *The British Table: A New Look at the Traditional Cooking of England, Scotland and Wales* (New York: Abrams, 2016).
[4] Robin McDouall, *The Gourmet's London* (New York: HarperCollins, 1969).
[5] Alan Bennett, 'The Stringalongs', *London Review of Books*, 16/24 (24 February 1994).
[6] Ibid.
[7] Terence Conran, *Printed Textile Design* (London: Studio Publications, 1957), 67.
[8] Ibid.
[9] Ibid., 93.
[10] Ibid., 77.

Tastemaking

TERENCE CONRAN — MAKING MODERN BRITAIN

Terence had seen the Svenskt Tenn store in Stockholm, as well as Den Permanente and Illums Bolighus in Copenhagen on his trips to Scandinavia in the 1950s. They offered exemplary ranges of modern furniture. Their displays mixed Artek tables and Hans Wegner chairs with fabrics by Marimekko and glass by Carlo Scarpa. In America, the architects Ben and Jane Thompson had opened the Design Research store in Cambridge, Massachusetts, as early as 1953 and filled it with Eames aluminium group chairs, George Nelson's clocks, Alexander Girard textiles and Florence Knoll tables. There were no such places in Britain. Habitat, Terence's idea for a new shop that first began to take shape in 1963, would be a pioneer, doing for chairs what Mary Quant had done for the miniskirt and what Barbara Hulanicki would do for purple tights at Biba. It would change not just the way that people bought furniture, but also how they used it.

As Terence saw it, the people who bought their clothes at Bazaar and Biba would be his natural customers. The first Habitat, which opened in May 1964, set out to be a place attractive enough for people to go there on a Saturday ready to be entertained. There would be unexpected things for them to see and touch, as if they were going to a gallery or an exhibition. This reflected lessons about retailing that Terence had learned from Simpson and the work there of Natasha Kroll. There would be a sound system to play the Beatles. Eventually, there would be a café. With his gift for finding neighbourhoods that were not yet fashionable, Terence rented a ground floor with a basement at the top end of the Fulham Road, just across the street from the Michelin garage that he would be able to buy twenty years later.

He knew that he would have to sell more than high-priced, once-in-a-lifetime purchases such as beds, sofas and dining tables. There would be plenty of rapid-turnover, impulse buys to tempt people and to keep them coming back. And there would need to be more affordable versions of some of those expensive pieces if the place was not to become forbidding.

Just before the opening, the fashion photographer Terence Donovan took a series of pictures of Terence and his team for *The Sunday Times* that distilled the essence of Habitat's appeal and caught most, but not all, of the people responsible for setting it up. Under the headline 'What the Smart Chicks are Buying', the paper published a different version of Donovan's much-better-known image in which Terence, a little plumper than in his student days, is standing at the centre of the picture. His hair is neatly trimmed, the whole team having just come back from a session at Vidal Sassoon. He is wearing a jacket and tie over his authentic and pristine butcher's apron specially purchased from a Smithfield supplier for the opening-night party. His left hand is resting on a replica of an antique enamel bin, salvaged from a fish-and-chip shop, that carries the legend 'HOT SAVELOYS' in a florid Victorian script. The bin is balanced on the cane seat of a Thonet bentwood chair. Next to it is a Habitat-branded shopping bag, which formed a walking advertising campaign in bold type and proclaimed kitchen goods, fabrics, carpets,

The first Habitat store, with its characteristic white brick walls

Inspired by French markets, merchandise was piled high

china, glass and furniture. It was the work of Virginia Clive-Smith, a talented graphic designer who worked at Conran's studio in Hanway Place, but was also involved with the early issues of the underground magazine *Oz*. Clive-Smith was responsible for the cover of issue 8 from January 1968, which showed the impact of the fascination for Day-Glo colours and psychedelia of the period on conventional graphic design.

The Conran studio was attracting other designers with similar interests at the time. Colin Fulcher, who transformed himself into Barney Bubbles, worked there from 1965 and, aside from his designs for Habitat and Terence's commercial clients

TASTEMAKING

Three versions of a living room furnished with items from the Habitat range from 1965, before the acquisition of Lupton Morton, manufacturers of Campus furniture, and their mail-order expertise. There were already signs of the art direction that would characterise the Habitat catalogue, using props that establish the design credentials of the products shown. The record player in the bottom room set, for example, is Dieter Ram's SK 4 for Braun, the so-called 'Snow White's coffin'

147

in the office, produced a series of remarkable music projects including Hawkwind's album cover for *In Search of Space*, a logo for Ian Dury and the artwork for Elvis Costello's *Almost Blue*.

Caroline Conran is seated in the foreground of Donovan's carefully composed picture in a chic dress with ruffled collar and cuffs that she designed herself. She has the London look of the early 1960s: modern, stylish and beautiful – and showing no sign that she is pregnant with her first child. Philip Pollock is standing to Terence's left in a full-length butcher's striped apron, hand on hip, wearing thick glasses and an unmistakable smirk that *Private Eye* immediately parodied. Also in the picture are Pagan Taylor, glamorous in a sleeveless dress and proper shoes, Kate Currie and Sonja Jarman. They are standing in front of a white wall on which the word Habitat has been rendered in white Baskerville letters that were low-relief and three-feet high, all in lower case – an affectation that references Bauhaus practice. In fact, the Habitat logo was the work of Dudley Bootes-Johns, another graphic designer in the Conran studio.

Like Nigel Henderson's authoritative photograph of the Smithsons and Eduardo Paolozzi, taken on a Chelsea street eight years earlier for *This is Tomorrow*, the image seems to be saying 'these are the people who know that something new and significant is going on'. Missing from Donovan's picture are Oliver Gregory, a long-time employee of Terence's, who gave the shop its slatted ceiling, white-painted brick walls and robust floor tiles. He and Pagan Taylor would get married later, but the relationship did not last. Also missing is Maurice Libby, who planned the displays that set out to capture the generosity of French street markets, with objects piled high. It was never just one pillar-box red teapot for Habitat, but a stack of them reaching all the way to the ceiling. This was an approach that helpfully did away with the need for a separate stock room.

While Habitat was still in the planning stages, Terence had met and married his third wife, Caroline Herbert. They would have three children: Tom, Sophie and Ned. After art school in Cambridge, Caroline had worked for *House and Garden*, and had become the home editor for *Queen* magazine. By the time she met Terence she was building her career as a food writer. With French fluent enough to translate Michel Guérard's books as well as those of other chefs, she had just the right combination of talents needed both to shape Habitat's extensive cookware ranges and to write copy for its catalogues.

Sonja Jarman had been a buyer at Liberty before working for Conran and Co. Kate Currie and Maurice Libby had both worked for Woolland Brothers, a defunct Knightsbridge department store belonging to the Debenhams Group that had once stood next to Harvey Nichols. The furniture department, the most stylish in London at the time, had sold a lot of Terence's products. Habitat opened just as Debenhams had decided to close Woolland Brothers and sell the building for redevelopment. Terence recruited several of its staff.

Pollock, who owned a bed- and sofa-making company called Aerofoam, invested in Habitat when Terence failed to raise a bank loan. Pagan Taylor, the former model photographed by Tony Snowdon for *Vogue* in New York, with her ex-husband, the architect John Taylor, whose firm designed New Scotland Yard in Victoria Street, also invested in the shop, as did Caroline. Taylor was the public face of the shop, credited with coming up with the Habitat name from the pages of a thesaurus and described as its managing director, in a move partly designed to keep Terence's existing network of retailers from seeing him as too much of a competitor.

For the first time Terence was selling directly to the public, rather than the well-informed community of architects and designers who specified his furniture for their buildings, or to the retailers. He had no choice. Having opened his Thetford factory a year earlier, he had boosted his capacity substantially. But orders from Britain's furniture retailers, who were mostly sceptical about Terence's taste for modernity, had not increased proportionately. He was going to have to bypass the gatekeepers and become a retailer himself if he wanted to keep the factory going.

Terence had always talked about Habitat as a nationwide chain, and the runaway success of the first Fulham Road store made that a real possibility. He finally got a bank loan, bought out Taylor and Pollock, and opened a second Habitat in Tottenham Court Road, near Heal's, the shop he had been so impressed by in his childhood, which by this time was looking past its best. Further branches followed in Manchester and Glasgow, and the total number of stores in Britain, Europe and America, where for trademark reasons they were called Conran's, eventually reached more than eighty.

Initially Terence planned to fund the expansion by selling a stake in the store to a larger partner. There was an approach from Reed, the paper group, that came to nothing. Then, at the end of 1968, just four years after the first Habitat opened, the Conran businesses merged with Ryman, a publicly quoted company that specialised in office supplies and stationery. The architect Brian Henderson, a partner in the firm YRM, and his wife Elizabeth Henderson, parents of the chef Fergus Henderson, had both worked for Ryman, and introduced Maurice Ryman to Terence. The deal was brokered by Morgan Grenfell, the merchant bank at which Roger Seelig was head of corporate finance. Seelig and Morgan Grenfell would later play a large part in the financial engineering that enabled Terence to acquire Mothercare and create Storehouse.

TERENCE CONRAN   MAKING MODERN BRITAIN

TASTEMAKING

Terence Donovan's famous photograph of the Habitat team taken just before the opening of the first shop on London's Fulham Road in 1964 caught the moment when Britain's domestic tastes were about to go through a sudden change

The Ryman–Conran merger was not a success. The two Ryman brothers saw the Habitat shops as a distraction, and believed that the merged business should focus on the more valuable contract market. It took Terence eighteen months to get out of the deal and it was an abrupt and painful severance. He had raised enough money from a merchant bank to buy Habitat back, but the design studio, the contract businesses and the factory in Thetford stayed with Ryman.

For Terence, the point of the merger had been to raise the money he needed to expand Habitat around the world. He found other ways to grow that business when he bought the Habitat stores back from Ryman, and embarked on plans for floating them that finally came to fulfilment in 1981.

Terence moved his remaining team out of Hanway Place and into Neal Street in Covent Garden. Rodney Fitch, senior member of the studio, who had worked with him on the second branch of Habitat, chose to stay. But there was nothing in the agreement to stop Terence from starting a new design consultancy which he immediately did under the name Conran Associates. Ryman itself kept the name Conran Design Group, an organisation which still exists but which has had no connection with Terence since he sold his shares in Ryman.

Ryman itself was soon to be swallowed by the Burton Group, and Fitch set up his own business, Fitch and Co., which would become one of the largest design consultancies in the world during the design boom of the 1980s.

But in two respects, the brief merger had benefited Terence. His shares in Ryman gave him a windfall profit when the company was sold to Burton, and he retained control of Lupton Morton. Ryman had acquired the business of Tom Lupton and John Morton, a furniture manufacturer, in 1969. They had a factory employing 100 people in Wallingford, larger than Conran's Thetford operation, and solid experience of using mail-order catalogue sales to expand their domestic market beyond furnishing student halls of residence. And Terence retained control of the Wallingford operation when he bought back Habitat.

Morton and Lupton met as students at the Architectural Association. After working for Robert Goodden and RD Russell on the Lion and Unicorn pavilion at the Festival of Britain, they set up in practice together, working on an eclectic range of projects that involved architecture, a property company called Townmaker with the engineer Tony Hunt and the architect Tom Hancock, and furniture, which was the most successful.

Morton designed the impressive Campus range of furniture, targeted at the massive expansion of the new universities in the 1960s. They equipped a score of universities with self-assembly flat-pack furniture as student numbers doubled in Britain. Lupton Morton began advertising its range in *The Sunday Times* colour

CONRAN FURNITURE

Catalogues were an essential part of Terence's marketing strategy from as early as the 1950s. The Conran furniture range was initially presented in a set of simple drawings. The graphic designer Ian Bradbery created a more sophisticated look

supplement, offering sales direct from the factory, and producing a mail-order catalogue designed by Derek Birdsall.

The Campus range continued in production under the new ownership, and Terence built on Lupton Morton's experience in mail order to create the Habitat catalogue. It turned out to be much more than a sales tool. Under Terence's direction the Habitat catalogues came to exert a powerful influence on Britain's domestic tastes.

Almost from the start of his career Terence was using catalogues to present his products. His first wife, Brenda Davison, put her architectural skills to work to help him to make a simple illustrated sheet setting out the range of tables and storage units, such as the options for his S1 cabinet. They included shelves and sliding doors that came in black, white and natural timber finishes. The sheet was little more than simple descriptions of individual pieces and a price list.

As Terence's range of furniture expanded, the catalogues became more sophisticated. The 1958 version, art directed by Ian Bradbery – a graphic designer Terence had known since he was at the Central School, and who was becoming recognised for his album covers for Lonnie Donegan's skiffle group, Big Bill Broonzy and Chris Barber, among others – ran to sixteen pages.

Terence did something more elaborate for the Summa range, which he started manufacturing in his Thetford factory. He created room sets, with judiciously placed design-conscious props such as a Braun portable radio, and Vico Magistretti's recently designed Carimate chair.

This was followed by a basic broadsheet-format Habitat catalogue, published for the first time in 1965. Caroline wrote the copy, and Juliet Glynn-Smith, who later became head of the Habitat design group, illustrated it. The catalogue turned into a creative project all of its own after 1969, an intricately plotted and orchestrated guided tour of Terence's world, offered as a highly desirable model for a way of life for others to follow. It was carefully photographed, making increasing use of real-life locations rather than room sets, and the items for sale were mixed with suggestive props. It often showed Terence's own homes at Dalham in Norfolk and St Andrews Place in London, increasing the sense that the catalogue was sharing a set of personal insights.

The catalogue made the whole mean more than the sum of its parts. It had the effect of creating a halo for every piece it showed, and acted as a prelude to the physical Habitat stores. Just as the department stores of the nineteenth century had shown the prosperous new bourgeoisie how to live, so the Habitat catalogue explained, without labouring the point, how modern life in the newly affluent Britain of the 1960s could be lived differently.

The first edition had a print run of 300,000 copies, and in later years this grew to as many as 1.5 million copies. The mix of products and ideas, art and food, furniture and cutlery, paint and textiles was far more powerful than the room sets that Terence had seen at the Festival of Britain. It was so compelling that he could distribute the catalogue in newsagents throughout Britain, and charge for it. The annual catalogue became the starting point for Conran's books about the domestic landscape, beginning with *The House Book*, which went into ten

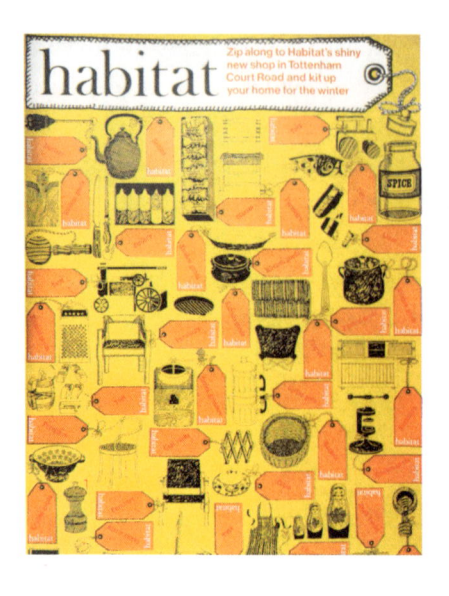

The opening of Habitat's second store on London's Tottenham Court Road was the starting point for an advertising campaign. In the early days, Habitat's image was shaped by the use of illustrations rather than photography

TASTEMAKING

By the time that Terence started making the Summa furniture range in Thetford, the catalogues were based on room sets, even though they were aimed at professionals

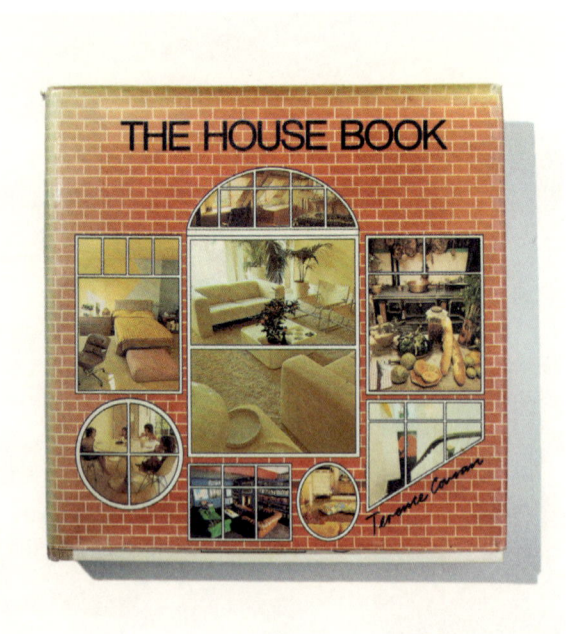

The success of *The House Book* encouraged Mitchell Beazley to produce other domestic titles. Terence later set up Conran Octopus, his own imprint with the publisher Paul Hamlyn, which created a whole list of books based on the Conran name

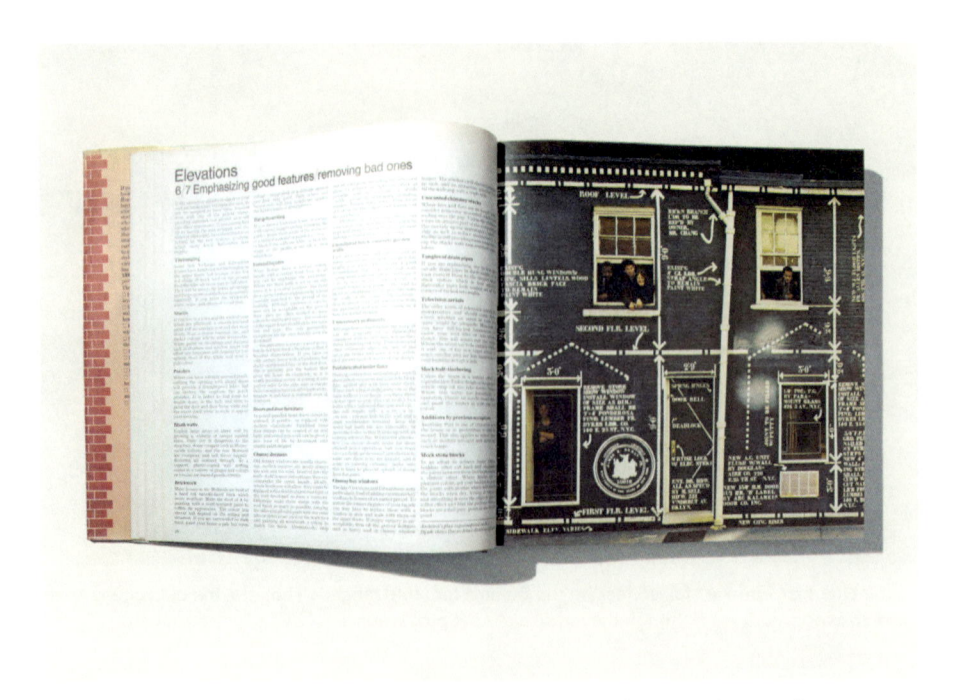

The House Book mixed practical advice with inspirational ideas, and a witty selection of images

editions between 1974 and 1983, and followed by successive publications on kitchens and bathrooms. Caroline, who became the food editor at *The Sunday Times*, where she embarked on the Campaign for Real Bread, started writing her own cookbooks – including the *Conran Cookbook*, which sold an astonishing million copies worldwide.

Together they had more impact on the image of aspirational domestic life in Britain in the twentieth century than any other single influence, at least until IKEA opened its first store in Warrington in 1987.

What made Terence stand out was his ability to create a way of life that other people wanted to share. The Habitat catalogues encapsulated it. *The House Book* laid it out as a canon. *The House Book*'s success persuaded Terence to start his own publishing imprint in partnership with Paul Hamlyn. Hamlyn was a German-born refugee who had married Helen Guest, a Royal College of Art graduate, and friend of Brian Henderson who made the introduction. Much as Thomas Chippendale had done in the eighteenth century, when he produced a portfolio of his designs titled *The Gentleman and Cabinet Maker's Director*, offering a family of pieces of furniture in a variety of styles that his clients could choose or adapt, so in the twentieth century the Habitat catalogue offered tables, chairs, beds and kitchenware, lights, wallpapers, rugs and fabrics that could be put together in multiple ways, in the confidence that they would work together.

Habitat catalogues encapsulated a modern world and made us all feel as if we were putting our noses to the window to peep in on somebody else's Christmas.

The 1971 catalogue assured readers:

It provides all you need to furnish a house in a way that is unmistakably of the 1970s without being either aggressively modern, or impossibly expensive. The colours are bright and clear, the style simple and fresh. But perhaps the most unique thing about this catalogue is that the whole range of merchandise is carefully coordinated. Therefore something you choose from page 2 will live happily with your choice from page 20, or even page 120.[1]

The props used in the photography were equally telling: in 1975 it was a white plastic Sony clock radio with clockwork numerals, and Giancarlo Piretti's folding steel and transparent plastic Plia chair. In 1977 it was Ettore Sottsass's red Valentine typewriter, made by Olivetti.

The catalogue provided everything for the home. It had the posters to frame for the walls of your living room in Islington in London, Byres Road in Glasgow,

From 1971, the Habitat catalogue became a creative project in its own right

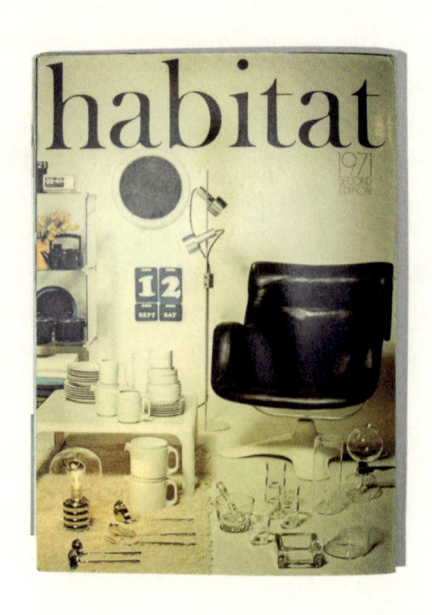

Early catalogues featured modern classics, from Yrjö Kukkapuro to Ingo Maurer

or Edinburgh's Stockbridge, and almost anywhere in Bath or Cambridge. You could choose from Toulouse-Lautrec advertising masked balls on Tuesdays and Saturdays at the Moulin Rouge, Howe tricycles as used by a Victorian gent in a pith helmet, or Alphonse Mucha's poster for Bières de la Meuse that brought a touch of florid Art Nouveau, a style that a younger Terence had dismissed as introverted and decadent. It would be lit by a framing spot, positioned on a Rotaflex Habitat track.

The catalogues sold a lot more than just furniture. The German consumer electronics company Braun, its products guided by Dieter Rams, was well represented. There was a personal desk fan, a cigarette lighter and a fan heater. These were products with a resonance that extended beyond their utilitarian purpose. Richard Hamilton once suggested that Rams's toaster for Braun had the same level of significance for him as Mont Sainte-Victoire had for Cézanne. This was going a little far, perhaps, but Hamilton was also prepared to satirise himself. He attached a set of false teeth to a Braun electric toothbrush, and titled it *The Critic Laughs*. A Braun product was a reflection of a certain set of attitudes in its owner, just as an Eames lounge chair was, or a Joe Colombo acrylic table, which was also available from Habitat for a while.

There was even a Habitat stereo system. According to the 1971 catalogue:

Now that stereophonic records are rapidly superseding mono, a stereo system is necessary for every music enthusiast. We found most tended to be either bleak pieces of machinery or large pieces of furniture with more wood and decoration than equipment, so we designed a system which would fit sensibly into any well-furnished modern home.

Unable to resist the temptation to blind customers with dubious science, the catalogue suggested that 'it takes up to eight records, has a four-speed player, and offered optional manual or automatic changer, six watts per channel, ganged potentiometer, minimal crosstalk between channels, and balance controls'.

The paint colours were particularly revealing of the era. The 1977 catalogue featured otter brown, café au lait, mint green and buttercup yellow. In 1973 there were spun aluminium lampshades, in six stunning colour combinations, all with a crisp white interior: coral, white, with an orange band, mustard and white, mustard and coral.

Unwittingly, the catalogue also provides a penetrating insight into the social prejudices of its time. Among the children's toys on offer in 1969 was the 'golliwog, the oldest toy in the cupboard, and still the most popular'. This was a time when the jam manufacturer Robertson's was distributing hundreds of thousands

Ryman-Conran's takeover of Lupton Morton brought the Campus range to Habitat

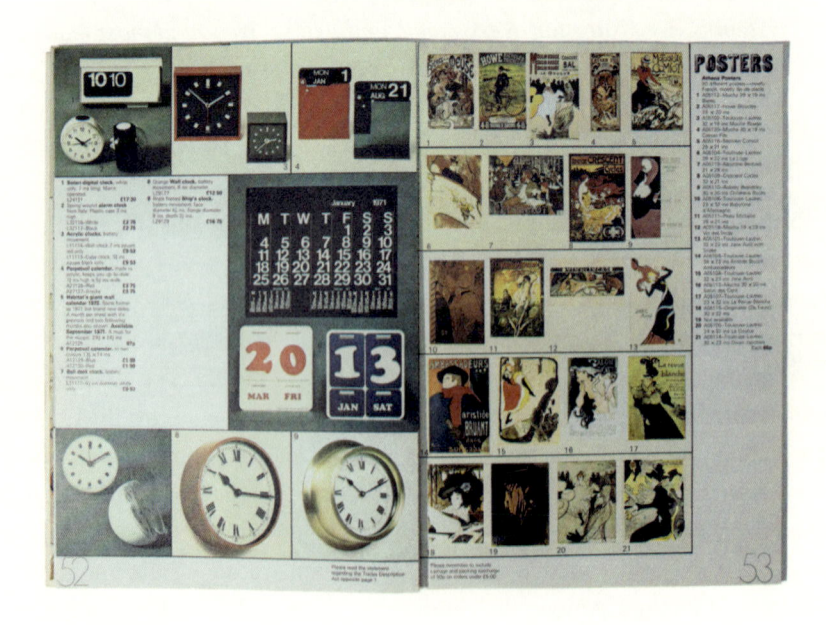

The posters that shaped a generation's living room walls came from Habitat

TERENCE CONRAN   MAKING MODERN BRITAIN

TASTEMAKING

The lighting range from 1971 reflected a very particular colour palette

Charles and Ray Eames, Eero Saarinen and Harry Bertoia designs featured as a kind of Design Museum in the catalogue

Dining Room

Stools. Solid elm. High and low.
F5030 27" high £5·70
F5031 18" low £5·00

Cypress. Wood chairs made in Yugoslavia. Thick rush seats. 38" × 15½" × 16".
F5193 £15·25

Magistretti chairs. Beech. Natural or red stained frame, rush seat.
Side chair 29" × 20" × 17".
F5190 natural, F5190 red £16·00
Arm chair 29" × 23" × 18".
F5191 natural, F5191 red £19·50

Quaker. Beech frame, string seat. 29" × 19" × 15½".
F5533 £18·75

Classic bentwood chair. Cane seat. 35" × 16" × 16".
F5175 white, F5175 natural £12·75

Bentwood side chair. Natural clear lacquered frame, cane seat and back. 31" × 17½" × 16".
F5179 £19·75

Bauhaus side chair. Chromed steel and black stained wooden frame, cane seat and back. 31" × 19" × 22½". F5711 £26·25

Bauhaus arm chair. 31" × 24" × 22½".
F5712 £32·25

Flexx. Chromed steel frame. Groovy corduroy upholstered seat. 32" × 17" × 14½". (See page 13 for Groovy and please put colour required on the order form). F5680 £24·50

GF40. Light stacking chair. Plastic coated steel skin seat and back, chromed frame. 30" × 19" × 20½".
F5630 white £13·82

Selene. Moulded fibreglass. Very strong. 30" × 18½".
F5082 £15·75

Stuns mini. Stretched canvas seat.
(See also pages 16-19)
31" × 19" × 20½".
F5470 orange, F5470 brown, F5470 green, F5470 yellow, F5470 black.
£11·00

TERENCE CONRAN   MAKING MODERN BRITAIN

TASTEMAKING

CHAIRS AND STOOLS

Director's chair. Folding beech frame, canvas seat and back. 35" × 22" × 18". F5253 natural canvas, F5253 indigo canvas £12·00

Folding chairs. Beechwood. Folds to 1⅜". 30" × 18" × 18". F5192 natural, F5192 red stained £5·25

Plia. Chromed frame, clear or smoky acrylic seat. 29¾" × 18¼" × 19". Folds to 2". F5290 clear, F5290 smoky £15·75

Stickback. Lacquered beech. Sold in sets of 4. 31" × 17" × 14½". F5252 red, F5252 yellow, F5252 white, per 4 £31·80

Faeroe. Natural beech frame. Groovy corduroy upholstered seat. 31" × 18¼" × 17¾". (See page 13 for Groovy and please write on the order form which colour you require). F5494 £19·50

Faeroe. Black stained beech frame, string seat. (See also pages 30/31). 31" × 18¼" × 17¾". F5494 £19·50

Portrayed both full face and in profile, Habitat's chair collection of what became the usual suspects for seating, including Thonet bentwood and tubular steel cantilevers inspired by Marcel Breuer. Terence's part in introducing the British to Italian design, in particular to Vico Magistretti's red Carimate chair with its rush seat (top row, third from the left) earned him a Compasso d'Oro for lifetime achievement from the Italian Industrial Design Association. For a while, Habitat also stocked Giancarlo Piretti's transparent Plia chair (top right) and David Rowlands' GF 40 (bottom row, fourth from left), as well as Magistretti's moulded plastic Selene chair (bottom row, fifth from left)

163

Consciously or unconsciously, the Habitat catalogue revealed the social prejudices and assumptions of its time. The company had a team of buyers finding toys for its selections, but with flower presses and miniature steam engines on offer, it's clear that in 1971 at least Terence himself had an important input

of enamel golliwog badges every year. By 1973 the golliwogs had disappeared, at least from the Habitat catalogue.

There were several items that clearly touched on Terence's own childhood memories: telescopes and flower presses, a pocket tent, bows and arrows, kites and a Mamod miniature steam traction engine.

Through the catalogue's pages it was even possible to track the state of Britain's economy. Its price lists reflected a period of rampant inflation in Britain, which peaked at almost twenty-five per cent in 1975. Habitat's regular best-seller, a remarkably cheap A-shaped folding beechwood dining chair, manufactured in Yugoslavia, was priced at £3.25 in 1972, went up to £5.25 in 1975, £7.50 in 1977, and had reached £10.75 by 1978 – its price trebling in five years.

Every year the catalogue offered a slightly different product range and editorial approach. By 1973, when Terence felt confident enough about the catalogue to charge 30p a copy, it was art directed by Stafford Cliff. Michael Wickham took the photographs, twenty years after that first trip that he and Terence took to France. The issue was a brilliant exercise in having it both ways. The front cover showed a fashionable glass-box living room with a young woman with a blonde pageboy cut, a blue-and-white striped top, and enormously wide-flared trousers in velvet, while the back was a matronly lady in a pinafore, with a kitchen table weighed down by turkey, lobster and madeira cake.

Inside it had smart design-world celebrities, partly for voyeuristic reasons, partly for reassurance, to give you an idea of how to put it all together, along with a Cartier-Bresson image of a picnic on the banks of the Marne. It represented an irresistible mix of what appears to be a technical manual, romantic aspiration, anticipation and celebrity gawking.

TASTEMAKING

The catalogue was desirable enough to support a cover price that increased from 30p to 85p

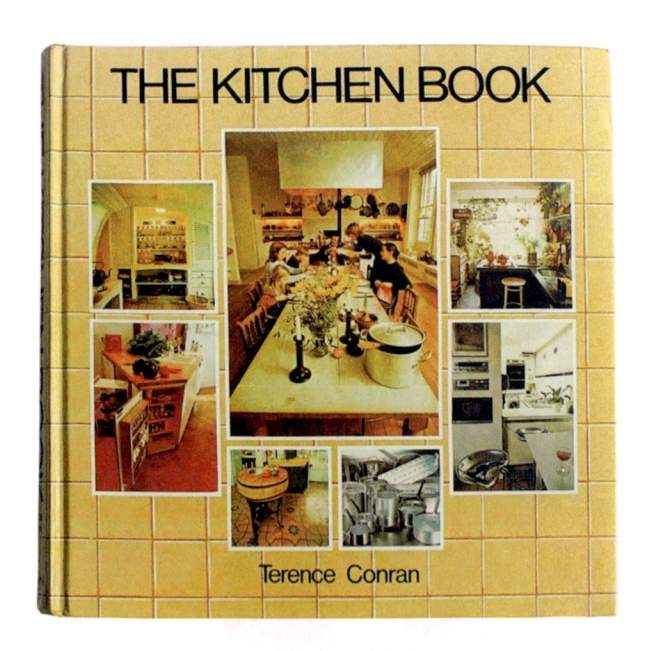

After the success of *The House Book*, the publishers used the same format to explore other aspects of domestic life, starting with the kitchen. It helped to consolidate the association of the brand with food

The Habitat catalogue enlisted Elizabeth David's help in putting together a selection of kitchenware that came with her endorsement

TERENCE CONRAN   MAKING MODERN BRITAIN

Enzo Apicella, who invented the look of the modern Italian restaurant for a London audience, is portrayed at a white circular table, on a white mesh Bertoia chair, on a white ceramic-tiled floor, with a flask of Chianti in a straw basket. He is wearing a tank top that makes him look like a Peter Blake portrait. Michael Chow, founder of the Knightsbridge restaurant Mr Chow, which combined dumplings and duck and pancakes with Italian waiters, stands in a room full of Rodney Kinsman's chromed-steel tube armchairs, sofas, tables and storage.

There was plenty of drink on offer: forty-pint home-brew beer packs in one year, and wine from the cellars of Justerini & Brooks, who offered Sancey Champagne by the dozen bottles, Amontillado, Niersteiner Domtal 1969 and Portuguese rosé. There wasn't much food, just Elsenham jam in six packs. But there was everything you needed to prepare it.

> *This year we have asked Elizabeth David, probably the world's most authoritative food and cookery writer, to contribute her own section to the Habitat catalogue. She has selected for Habitat customers a basic batterie de cuisine from the very best equipment made in France and all over the world. Not cheap, but Mrs David has sound reasons for her preferences, and explains them with conviction. Over the years Mrs David has been responsible for introducing many people to the fundamental equipment of cookery, to the pots and pans of provincial France, and to the once-neglected English traditions. This serves as an illustrated appendix to her own books.*[1]

Mrs David, as she was always known by those who wanted to pay their knowing respects to the legend of the British kitchen, and who was the granddaughter of a viscount, also made an appearance in Terence's follow-up to *The House Book*, *The Kitchen Book*, published in 1977. She alone of the professionals who took part declined to be photographed specially for the book: a likely sign of a certain reluctance. She is represented by an agency photo, and, unlike Michael Chow, Fay Maschler or Prue Leith, she does not appear in her actual home, but instead offers up what the book called 'her dream kitchen'. Describing it, she took a characteristically stern line:

> *I recoil from coloured tiles, and beflowered surfaces, and I don't want a lot of things coloured avocado and tangerine. And too much equipment is if anything worse than too little. I don't a bit covet the exotic gear dangling from hooks, the riot of clanking ironmongery, the armouries of*

knives, or the serried ranks of saucepans and all other carefully chosen symbols of culinary activity I see in so many photographs of chic kitchens. Pseuds corners I'm afraid. Many of them.[2]

But she selected an asparagus cooker, a stock pot, milk and paella pans, and an egg cocotte, and she put her name to a leaflet on cooking with Le Creuset.

In the 1971 catalogue, Terence's house in St Andrews Place was used for the bedroom shoot, where the duvet made its appearance for the first time. Habitat did not use the word at first, for fear of baffling its customers. Instead, it somewhat apologetically coined a new word: 'the Slumberdown', which it described as 'a marvellously cozy quilt that cuts the work of bed making to a minimum'. Such was the novelty, the catalogue felt obliged to spell out its use to 'take the place of top sheets, blankets and eiderdowns, simply shake and plump each morning. The lightweight pure down is especially suited for centrally heated houses. Until you have tried this method of making a bed, it is difficult to believe it could be so simple'. It took two more years until duvets were finally called by their name.

The 1971 Habitat catalogue celebrated tins of paint, brass ships' clocks and bentwood chairs. It sold Dorothee Becker's wall pocket storage system made by Ingo Maurer, Kartell plastic bins and umbrella stands, fondue party kits with recipes for *fondue Bourguignonne*, hurricane lamps and hammocks, Solari digital clocks and perpetual calendars.

On page eight you could see Terence's kitchen in the house that he bought in Norfolk to be close to the factory in Thetford that he no longer owned. There was glossy enamelware from Poland, crisply edged in black, and copies of the *Larousse Gastronomique*.

Britain pre-Habitat was a country that invested countless hours in bedmaking, with carefully folded sheets tucked over blankets. The Scandinavians did things differently, and Terence introduced the duvet to the British high street: tentatively at first, calling it 'The Slumberdown'

TASTEMAKING

Habitat's cooks calendars became an annual event, a chance for customers to buy a low cost means of establishing themselves as sophisticated consumers of food, while at the same time subtly advertising the store. Caroline Conran was responsible for the weekly menu in the 1974 version, but there were a range of others involved, including Lisa Kinsman, who focused on Asian food

The catalogue was used to convey the interconnections of Terence's world. One year the Plaza and Groovy seating ranges were photographed at the Kasmin Gallery on Bond Street, with a Richard Smith piece in full view on the wall behind them, with gallery and artist both fully credited. When the catalogue photographed the Neal Street Restaurant, in 1973, the address and phone number were helpfully supplied.

And almost as if it were his own guilty pleasure, Terence included three pages of products that were not made by Habitat and would be unlikely to sell well in order to 'illustrate a few very expensive, but beautiful examples of furniture, lighting and china that have become classics of our time'. This museum within a catalogue displayed five different lamps designed and made by Ingo Maurer including his surrealist giant light bulb, Edison; Eero Saarinen's snow-white fibreglass Tulip chair; Joe Colombo's white moulded plastic table made by Kartell; the David Rowlands GF 40/4 stacking chair; Bertoia's wire chair; and the Karuselli armchair designed in 1964 by the Finnish architect Yrjö Kukkapuro that Terence always had in his offices. There was also what the catalogue described as 'Victorian but still a classic': a black leather Chesterfield. To complete the collection there was a lounge chair and ottoman described as being by Charles Eames (Ray was not credited at the time). This last retails at almost £9,000 today, so it was quite a statement. But

169

it is a group that encapsulates the nature of Terence's points of reference. All that is missing is a handmade pot and a Thonet bentwood chair. Continuing this sense of the catalogue's unstated mission as a kind of museum of design in print, the 1978 edition included a history of the bentwood chair.

The ever-larger catalogue was the product of a significant investment in Habitat's mail-order activities, which the sale of his shares in Burton had given him the infrastructure to build up.

Price was an extremely sensitive issue for Habitat. The Eames loungers, the Braun electrical appliances, the Bertoia and Kukkapuro all disappeared from Habitat stores. Instead, Terence opened the Conran Shop in November 1973, in what had been the original Habitat at 77 Fulham Road, which maintained the flavour of Terence's museum within a catalogue. At Habitat the emphasis was increasingly on the basics.

> *We started Habitat in 1964. At first we were one small shop in the Fulham Road. We wanted to provide a reasonable alternative to furnishing shops up and down the high streets of England, we wanted to sell well-designed modern furniture that was also well-made, comfortable and at a price most people could afford. We wanted to sell all the other things you need to furnish a house that reflected the style of furniture and were also inexpensive. We collected together a range of traditional cooking equipment much of which has been rejected by other shops, because they mistakenly assumed it was old fashioned. We could not find many of the things we wanted to sell at a reasonable price, so we set about designing our own product.*[3]

Habitat meant more than furniture. At the beginning of the hi-fi boom, it was offering its own brand of stereo systems, alongside a range of consumer electronics from design-conscious manufacturers, including Braun

TASTEMAKING

When it became clear that the Eames lounger was beyond the means of most Habitat customers, the Conran Store opened to offer more affluent and more design-committed customers a product range that stayed closer to Terence's personal tastes

Just as retailers now need to find ways of keeping bricks-and-mortar shops alive, the catalogue was carefully pitched to remind customers of the Habitat stores: 'If you have enjoyed the catalogue and we certainly had fun putting it together, why not come shopping at Habitat branches where you'll find a great deal more than we could ever possibly put into one catalogue.'[4] The copy paints an enticing picture of exotica brought back from around the world to offer a physical experience.

> *Big splashy Marimekko prints from Finland, lots of nice prints and textiles, and delicately drawn English chintz and flowers ... We are very keen on cooking good food and eating it too. To fill your kitchen, we have chosen the very best from France, Italy, and England.*

> *Habitat take pride in making the most of modern production methods, adding distinctive individuality with artefacts from all over the world, bolts of brilliantly coloured and patterned rugs from Africa, handmade cotton from India, terracotta pots for geraniums from Singapore, hand thrown French jugs with a brown speckled glaze, rush matting from Vietnam, wicker baskets from China, toys from Russia, books from Bloomsbury and shelves brim full of every sort of glass you can imagine.*[5]

Habitat was a dream of a way of life for a generation, and one of the projects that Terence most enjoyed. But from 1989 onward he became increasingly detached from the business, losing control of it with his departure from Storehouse, of which by then it formed a part. Habitat in France is a separate business that continues to flourish, but in Britain it has been through a number of owners, including Ingvar Kamprad's IKEA, the company that managed to connect manufacturing and retailing on such a large scale that it could make genuinely affordable products in a way that such a comparatively modestly sized business as Habitat never could.

And the difficulty that both Terence and later owners of Habitat had in making a profit demonstrated the importance of the contract market.

Habitat began as the style of choice for the strapped-for-cash student and the young professional setting up home for the first time. Terence described them as 'young moderns with lively tastes'. In almost imperceptible stages the Habitat look elbowed aside what had gone before it to become the signature style of grown-up Britain. Terence's look migrated from the newly gentrified inner-city streets to become the ubiquitous uniform of stylishly affluent suburbia. Terence's foam sofas, plastic wastepaper baskets, Art Deco wallpaper, brushed aluminium up-lighters and rush matting helped a generation liberate itself from the bleak memories of their parents' world. He showed how the lingering taint of utility furniture from the era of coin-in-the-slot gas fires and bath times, limited to three inches of hot water per person, could be dispelled with a coat of orange paint, a floor sander and a scattering of dhurries.

In the photographs of his house in St Andrews Place, the living room is painted a careful shade of buttermilk. The floorboards are stripped back. In the background, a striking contemporary painting hangs over the original marble fireplace. A fire burns in the grate, fuelled by logs in an outsize wicker log basket. There is a Vico Magistretti-designed chair at the table, while the outsize sofa is flanked by a pair of Mies van der Rohe chairs and a flock of giant floor cushions, covered in striped fabric. A spot lamp sits on the coffee table.

Terence's style never fossilised. Look at the mid-1970s living room in his Regent's Park Terrace house and the double-height living space in the Dockland's loft he lived in on the top two floors of Michael and Patty Hopkins' building in Shad Thames. The sofas were tobacco-coloured leather and deliberately designed to evoke memories of clubland. A large model biplane hung from the roof light. There are still stripped wooden floors, this time out of maple. The strong colours and the countrified trimmings have disappeared but there is a brass telescope. Both are unmistakably of their moment, and, equally unmistakably, Terence interiors.

[1] Habitat, *Habitat Catalogue 1971: Second edition*, 1971.
[2] Elizabeth David, 'Dream Kitchen', in *The Kitchen Book*, ed. Terence Conran (Mitchell Beazley: London, 1977).
[3] Habitat, *Habitat Annual Catalogue*, 1973.
[4] Ibid.
[5] Ibid.

The big bang

From 1983, Terence based himself in a spacious office that he had designed on the top floor of the Heal's Building on Tottenham Court Road. He had moved there from his Neal Street studios after buying one of London's oldest furniture businesses with money that he had made from floating Habitat two years earlier. Six years later, in 1989, he would leave in painful circumstances after resigning as CEO of Storehouse, taking with him nothing more than his right to the use of his name, and, in 1990, ownership of the single Conran Shop in the Fulham Road.

This had been a period of explosive growth for Terence's businesses. For a moment he became the face of the Big Bang, the transformation of the rules by which the City of London operated, an abiding legacy of the Thatcher era. He took charge of British Home Stores (BHS) thanks to financial engineering, but did not have a majority shareholding. However, Terence was motivated by a genuine desire to find ways to run a company better, and to use his design studio to modernise a retail business.

It was characterised by the financial columnists as ending in failure. But judged by the standards of Philip Green, who later bought BHS, the largest constituent part of Storehouse, it had at least remained solvent under Terence's tenure. Green, having left a hole in the BHS pension fund, was persuaded to shore it up with £363 million, having sold it to a former bankrupt for £1. Terence had left BHS a viable enough business for Green to want to buy it for £200 million some years later.

The top floor of the Heal's Building was an unlikely setting for some of the most hard-fought takeover battles of the 1980s, but it had a special significance for Terence. Behind its stripped classical limestone facade, the Heal family had not only been selling furniture there, but they designed and manufactured it as well. Originally established in 1818, the company reached its peak under the leadership of Sir Ambrose Heal, who became chairman in 1913 and ran the business for forty years. Ambrose Heal was an accomplished designer of furniture in the Arts and Crafts tradition who had begun by training as an apprentice cabinetmaker. He was also a successful entrepreneur and, as a founder of the Design and Industries Association, an early advocate for the importance of design to Britain's economy. Heal was appointed a Royal Designer for Industry, and knighted.

Ambrose Heal modernised his company's products, moving away from over-ornate period pieces towards plain and simple styles. At the same time, he opened the Mansard Gallery in the building, with an exhibition programme that ranged from art by Picasso and Amedeo Modigliani to tubular steel furniture. It was a combination that Terence certainly identified with.

Heal demolished the company's original building in a major expansion that started in 1916. He commissioned his cousin, the talented Arts and Crafts architect Cecil Brewer, to design a palatial replacement. Sir Edward Maufe, who built Guildford Cathedral, extended Brewer's building in 1937 – at a time when Heal was having simultaneous affairs with the architect's wife Prudence and with Dodie Smith, the buyer for the toy department and future author of *101 Dalmatians*.

After Ambrose Heal's death in 1959, his heirs found it increasingly difficult to maintain the company's success. The store had a fashionable young competitor snapping at its ankles from the mid-1960s. Having already moved his showroom to Tottenham Court Road, Terence had borrowed enough money from Morgan Grenfell to open the second branch of Habitat a few doors up the road and started the advertising campaign for the new shop with the slogan 'Heel over to Habitat'. In the 1970s Heal's tried to compete by launching Buzz, a style-conscious new department aimed at the young – 'you won't get the Buzz anywhere else', as its advertising claimed. But it was far too late. Terence closed Buzz when he took control.

The Heal family first opened its furniture store at the beginning of the nineteenth century. Ambrose Heal embarked on a major expansion, rebuilding the Tottenham Court Road store, in what was for the time a progressive architectural style, modernising the product range and the displays

Terence was a non-executive director and later chairman at Hepworth, a long-established men's tailoring company. During his time there, he encouraged its expansion into womenswear by buying an existing chain of shops, and rebranding it as Next

The original Heal's model, which amounted to maintaining an integrated factory and store on a valuable Central London site, no longer made sense. The upholstery makers and the mattress stuffers were decanted to a new factory and Terence carried out a wholesale restructuring of the building, treating it a little like the Tokyo fashion buildings that he had seen in Japan. He created a family of shops in-shop, bringing in Habitat and Mothercare, and opening a flower concession run by Julia Lane, wife of the artist Howard Hodgkin and a friend of Caroline Conran.

Oliver Heal left the board. Cranks, a vegetarian restaurant, was evicted, along with Acsis the jewellers and Rosenthal china. Under Terence's leadership, the amount of floor space dedicated to Heal's was cut back to 45,000 square feet from 85,000 square feet, with Habitat taking just over 25,000, half of the freed-up space.

Terence carved his office out of what had been a warren of attic work rooms. There were no windows, or direct views out to the street, but his office – like those of all the other senior managers of not only Heal's, but the rest of his enterprises who also worked here – opened off a central atrium filled with plants and with a roof light, from which sunlight filtered in.

It was in this space that Terence underwent a metamorphosis, changing from a successful designer and manufacturer who owned an equally successful furniture shop into one of the quintessential businessmen of the 1980s. He had already become a non-executive member of the board of Hepworth in 1979, and was its chair from 1981 to 1983, when he steered it to buy the Kendall chain of 600 womenswear shops and rebrand it as Next. Conran Associates designed a new look for the shops, and Terence recruited George Davies, a dentist-turned-retailer, to run the new business. The experience clearly left Terence with an understanding of the potential to create new and more interesting high-street brands from the ashes of their time-expired predecessors.

Alistair McAlpine, the Conservative Party treasurer, became a conduit to Margaret Thatcher and the government

Despite the antipathy that Terence often expressed towards Margaret Thatcher, there were aspects of her policies that he appreciated. For a man who was impatient with red tape and restrictions, life became easier after she came to power in 1979. Her policies, at the cost of three million unemployed for several years in a row, did tame the runaway inflation that had scarred the 1970s. And the prime minister was a ready listener when Terence petitioned her as one of the most high-profile retailers campaigning for an end to restrictions on Sunday trading. The Big Bang rewriting of the London Stock Exchange's rules occurred after Terence floated Habitat, but it turned on a tap of money which fuelled the expansion drive that enabled him to buy Mothercare. Terence's decision to buy Mothercare was a major turning point. Habitat was rooted in territory that he knew intimately. As a somewhat distant parent, baby products and children's clothes were far less familiar territory for him. Caroline unsuccessfully urged him to drop the idea. Terence wanted to show that he could make a success of a large business.

Margaret Thatcher certainly endorsed Terence. She approved his knighthood in the 1983 New Year's Honours List, which he received at Buckingham Palace from the Queen later that year. Alistair McAlpine, who was close to Terence and invested in the Butler's Wharf project, was certainly a conduit between them. Like Terence, McAlpine was a collector.

McAlpine was a favourite of Thatcher's despite his unpredictable taste for books and fine art. When she came to power in 1979, she appointed him deputy party chairman, a role he retained until 1983, and also honorary treasurer of the Conservative Party, its chief fundraiser – a position he filled until 1990.

It was in his room at Heal's that Terence celebrated the day in January 1986 that he became the chairman of his newly named holding company Storehouse, having merged Habitat Mothercare with British Home Stores to form it. No doubt by coincidence, Storehouse was also the name of a cottage in Essex where Terence had designed and built a kitchen in the 1950s for its owners Richard 'Dickie' Chopping and Denis Wirth-Miller, close friends of Francis Bacon. Chopping had taught in the ceramics department under David Queensberry at the Royal College of Art.

Terence had come a very long way. In three years, he went from running Habitat, with sales of £67 million, to Storehouse, with sales of £1 billion. It was in this same room at the top of Heal's that Terence turned down the chance to make himself £132 million, when he rejected an uninvited bid in September 1987 from Tony Clegg's property company, Mountleigh, that offered £1.8 billion for the Storehouse company. He was following the advice of Roger Seelig from Morgan Grenfell, who had served him well when he had previously suggested that Terence reject an offer from the American businessman Selim Zilkha, who owned Mothercare, when Terence was planning to float Habitat on the stock market. Rather than go through the complexities and uncertainties of a public share offering, Zilkha proposed to buy Habitat outright for £28 million. Seelig believed that Terence could do better if he turned the offer down, and he was proved right. Although rejecting Zilkha's bid did mean that the flotation of Habitat, first considered in 1978, took three years to achieve.

Habitat was valued at £57 million at the end of the first day's trading in 1981. Terence still owned at least seventy-five per cent of the company. The fusion of Terence's style-conscious retailing and his design studio with Mothercare's distribution system and its market proved highly successful. Sebastian Conran designed new products, including a folding pushchair, and Jasper Conran worked on maternity clothing lines. Profits and market share grew.

Terence felt he could repeat the strategy on an even bigger scale; Seelig thought so too, and knew how to find the money to do so. There were two giants on Britain's high streets, each with their own character, that seemed like promising targets for upstart retailers looking to take over organisations that had lost their way: Debenhams, a chain of department stores, and British Home Stores, which had its roots in a more affordable market.

The high street was changing rapidly. Terence's work at Habitat and Mothercare was one aspect of that change. Ralph Halpern's transformation of Burton, an established men's ready-to-wear suit manufacturer, into fashion-conscious Top Shop was another.

Halpern and Terence were both embarking on further expansion. Both could help each other, but they could also find themselves in competition for acquisitions. Halpern looked at both BHS and Debenhams, and decided, with some

After Habitat bought Mothercare, new clothing ranges were introduced

Sebastian Conran designed an ingenious folding pushchair for Mothercare

encouragement from Terence, to make the latter his target. Halpern's model was the fashion-building strategy that Terence was trying at Heal's. Halpern would use the floor space to bring in other brands, not as a range of items on a rail, but as independent entities. Terence offered to help by taking space for his own brands, and in the process profit from the fees that his design studio could earn by giving Halpern's properties a facelift.

With Halpern and Burton focused on Debenhams, Terence and Seelig set about constructing the financial architecture of a merger that would give him control of British Home Stores. It was a move that, had it succeeded, would have made Terence a billionaire.

Turning down an unsolicited offer turned out much less profitable than it had been for the Habitat flotation. Six weeks after the offer from Mountleigh was rejected, Wall Street crashed by twenty-two per cent in a single week's trading. Even more dangerously, sentiment in London turned against the Storehouse plan to revitalise BHS.

What had worked well at Habitat Mothercare, because Terence had ultimate control, did not work as well or as quickly at BHS, where he struggled to assert his authority. BHS veterans such as Denis Cassidy found themselves in conflict with the people Terence appointed. Mostly they were the team that he had relied on in his previous businesses. In the face of an economic downturn, BHS failed to meet the financial targets investors expected. Cassidy resigned and then the takeover bids began, with predators scenting an opportunity.

Mountleigh's offer would have given real financial commitment. It was followed by Benlox, a more speculative approach two months later, whose £2 billion offer involved more paper shares than cash. Yet another bid came the following year from the American raider Asher Edelman. As a result, Terence spent more of his energies in the two years following Mountleigh's bid fighting off hostile takeovers. These raiders were seeking to break up the pieces and make a profit more than they were focusing on updating BHS, which was rebranded and reconfigured. Food was loss-making, and dropped from the mix.

Seelig had a lot on his mind too. In 1986 Morgan Grenfell was also working on another takeover, helping Guinness to buy the Distillers Company. This became a cause célèbre, a case study in the excess of the deal-making culture of the period, when it became clear that Guinness had prevailed in the takeover through artificially inflating its own share price by lending its allies the money to buy shares. It was an illegal act that led to two waves of prosecutions: a jail sentence for Gerald Ronson, and the arrest of Roger Seelig for stock manipulation. Terence Conran and Paul Hamlyn stood as sureties for his £250,000 bail before the trial collapsed in 1992. Seelig was judged innocent of the scandal and retired to Upton House, his impressively remodelled Cotswold country home.

Terence was forced into finding ways to maintain Storehouse's share price. The company sold its stake in the SavaCentre business to its partner Sainsbury in March 1989, and also its twenty per cent share of the French book retailer Fnac. Gradually the people that Terence had appointed – from the BHS chief executive Geoff Davey, who he brought over from Habitat, to his sister Priscilla, who was a Habitat buyer – were sacked or moved sideways. Finally, the board appointed an American retailer, David Dworkin, against Terence's wishes on a £400,000 salary. This was huge for its day, with stock options that could make him a further £4 million. His first act was to cull 900 jobs.

The successful transformation of Mothercare pushed Terence to attempt to repeat the process on an even larger scale. Habitat Mothercare merged with the dowdy department store chain British Home Stores. A new logo was the first step in a rebranding campaign, along with a new look for the shops and an investment in new product lines

Terence designed his own office when he moved into the Heal's building

This was still a profitable business, with what seemed to be a promising future. And the British high street then was a very different place from what it has become today. Out-of-town shopping in big malls had yet to take hold, still less the devastating impact of internet retailing that would, within the course of the pandemic year of 2021, see both Debenhams and Top Shop crash into insolvency and leave hundreds of stores empty.

In Terence's Heal's office there was barely a trace of the turmoil of the 1980s. The plain wood desk at which he sat in an Eames soft-pad chair with cast aluminium arms, upholstered in black leather, never had a computer on it. In fact, Terence would never learn to use one or even to send an email or read a text. There was a telephone, a Tizio desk light, designed by Richard Sapper and the signature at the time of a modern workplace, and usually a small ceramic vase that contained a dozen white tulips. There might also be the most recent copy of the Habitat catalogue, placed tidily alongside a neat stack of documents that he was working on, the Olivetti desk diary that he used to track his appointments, a couple of photographers' loops used for examining slides, and a small light box. He kept the magazines that he was reading here too: usually a copy of *House and Garden*, alongside *Blueprint* magazine. There might also be *Elle Decoration* and *World of Interiors*. There was always a ruler and a felt pen and a circular ashtray, usually with a Havana cigar. There was a kilim on the floor, a leather sofa designed by Antonio Citterio, and a fragment of stained glass showing the Michelin Man's head and shoulders, which Terence was planning to install in the Michelin building on Fulham Road that he bought in partnership with the publisher Paul Hamlyn.

Across the room squatted an Yrjö Kukkapuro Karuselli armchair. And, in a conspicuous hint to visitors about the design mission of the room's occupant, there also stood a drawing board. It had a black Heron Parigi stool pulled up for use, and a wicker basket bursting with rolls of tracing paper. It looks like a carefully curated image: the forlorn and unused drawing board tells us that this is not the workplace of somebody who wants to be considered as the conventional CEO of a FTSE 100 company. But nor is it that of a fulfilled man. Terence was never able to use that drawing board for the purpose for which it was intended.

For a short period, in this room, Terence was attempting to maintain control not just of the eighty or so Habitat outlets around the world, which by now included franchises in Japan (the Seibu department store had started franchising the Habitat name after 1982), a separate operation in France and mainland Europe and in America, but also of several hundred branches of British Home Stores, all the Mothercare shops, and the acquisitions made by Storehouse, the Richard Shops, the Blazer chain and Heal's. This was to say nothing of his half-stake in Conran

Octopus, of Conran Associates and of his property developments at Butler's Wharf. He was also building the Design Museum at Shad Thames and starting Benchmark. There was no more time to design chairs, to collect butterflies, or to cook.

It was an experience that left Terence reflective.

The way I first lost control of Habitat and then became removed from the business altogether was easily the saddest and most depressing time of my life. As we created a retail giant in Storehouse, it became too big to control or allow me the day-to-day personal involvement that gave me so much pleasure. It was a political log jam. I hadn't designed any furniture for near-enough a decade.

While losing Habitat felt like the death of a much-loved family member, the money I had made from it allowed me to start a bright and exciting new chapter in my life and create a restaurant group, focus on The Conran Shop and get designing again.[1]

Terence left his office in Heal's in 1989 and moved to Butler's Wharf, handing it over to Michael Julien, the former finance director of Guinness who took his place as chief executive, an appointment made on the advice of Seelig. Terence remained as chairman of Storehouse until 1990. Even though Terence lost control of Storehouse and Butler's Wharf almost at the same time, unlike at the Heal's Building he left a permanent trace of his work in Shad Thames with Fred Lloyd Roche.

Roche was a sophisticated architectural professional who had been the chief executive of the Milton Keynes Development Corporation for ten years. He implemented the laissez-faire planning strategy of building a city where people wanted to be, rather than forcing them to go somewhere they didn't. Milton Keynes was situated midway between London and Birmingham, next to the M1 motorway. It had its own new station on the mainline from Euston to Birmingham New Street.

Roche built up an impressive architecture and planning team, as well as commissioning architects of the quality of Norman Foster. He had previously commissioned James Stirling at Warrington New Town. After ten years, with the main elements of Milton Keynes in place, Roche decided to set up on his own, and brought with him a substantial proportion of his team from Milton Keynes, including the architect Stuart Mosscrop and the planner Lee Shostak.

One of Conran Roche's first major projects came about as the result of a boat trip that Terence took down the Thames in 1981. He spotted that only a few of the

THE BIG BANG

The warehouses of Butler's Wharf transformed into apartments, with restaurants at ground level

Designed by Michael and Patty Hopkins for David Mellor, the Conran studio moved here

Shad Thames as it had once been

Built on Shad Thames in the 1950s, this banana-ripening warehouse would be transformed into the Design Museum

nineteenth-century brick buildings that trailed eastwards from Tower Bridge along the south bank were occupied. The owner, P&O, was renting these on short-term lets as artists' studios. It is where Andrew Logan staged the notorious Alternative Miss World competition. Only two or three streets back from the river was some of the most deprived social housing in Britain.

Terence's boat trip took place in the year that the last of London's upstream docks, the Royal Docks, closed. It was the final act in a process of continuous decline, triggered by the invention of the shipping container, that had started when the East India Docks shut down in 1967. When Terence saw it, there was a full seven miles of continuous dereliction on both riverbanks all the way from Tower Bridge to Beckton. The ships that once clustered around the wharves and the 25,000 jobs that went with them had evaporated.

When Terence and Roche went for a walk down Shad Thames, they found a neighbourhood as deserted as the Covent Garden in which Terence had founded the Garage at the start of the 1970s. There was the residual scent of spices in the air. Shad Thames itself was a crevice of a street between brick cliffs of warehouses criss-crossed by cast-iron bridges, and was a powerful reminder of what the docks had once been.

In 1981, when Michael Heseltine, then the environment minister, embarked on a massive experiment by taking the area out of the hands of local government, it wasn't just London's docks that were dying. The capital itself had been haemorrhaging people for half a century. At 6.6 million, London's population was the lowest it had been since before the First World War, two million fewer than at its peak.

Tower Hamlets, Southwark and Newham were stripped of their planning powers in the 5,100 acres placed under the control of the London Docklands Development Corporation (LDDC). Heseltine appointed Reg Ward, who had come from running Irvine New Town in Scotland, as its chief executive. Ward had an £80 million-a-year budget with which to attract private investment into the area, and a barrage of incentives to offer. He established the Isle of Dogs Enterprise Zone with no land tax, no training levies, no planning restrictions, a 100 per cent tax write-off on capital costs and a ten-year tax holiday.

Terence bought the Butler's Wharf land at just the right moment from P&O, its former owner, whose previous attempts at redevelopment had all been thwarted by Southwark. With Southwark removed from the planning process, development immediately became easier. The LDDC had control and was open to private-sector proposals for how to handle the void.

TERENCE CONRAN   MAKING MODERN BRITAIN

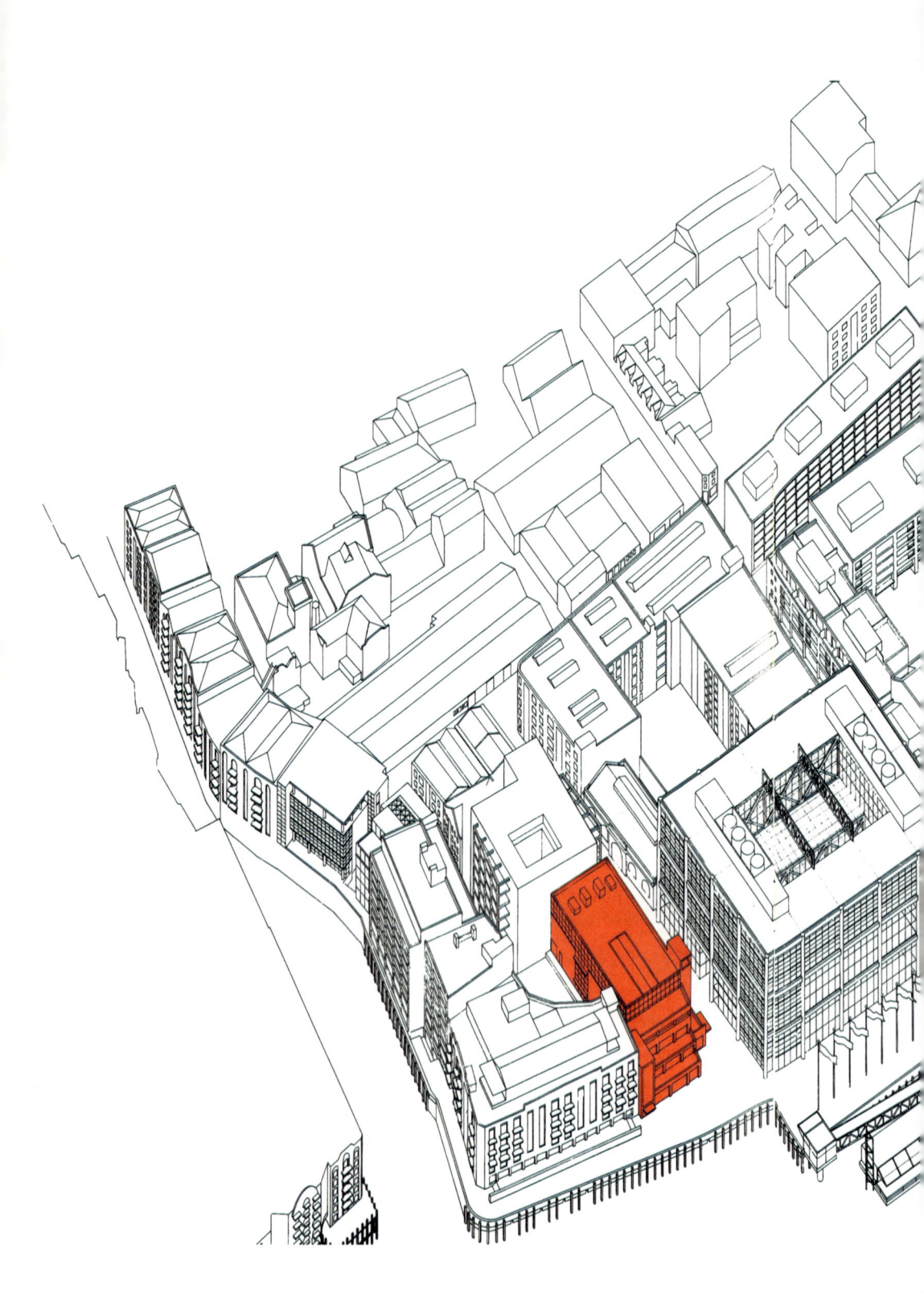

THE BIG BANG

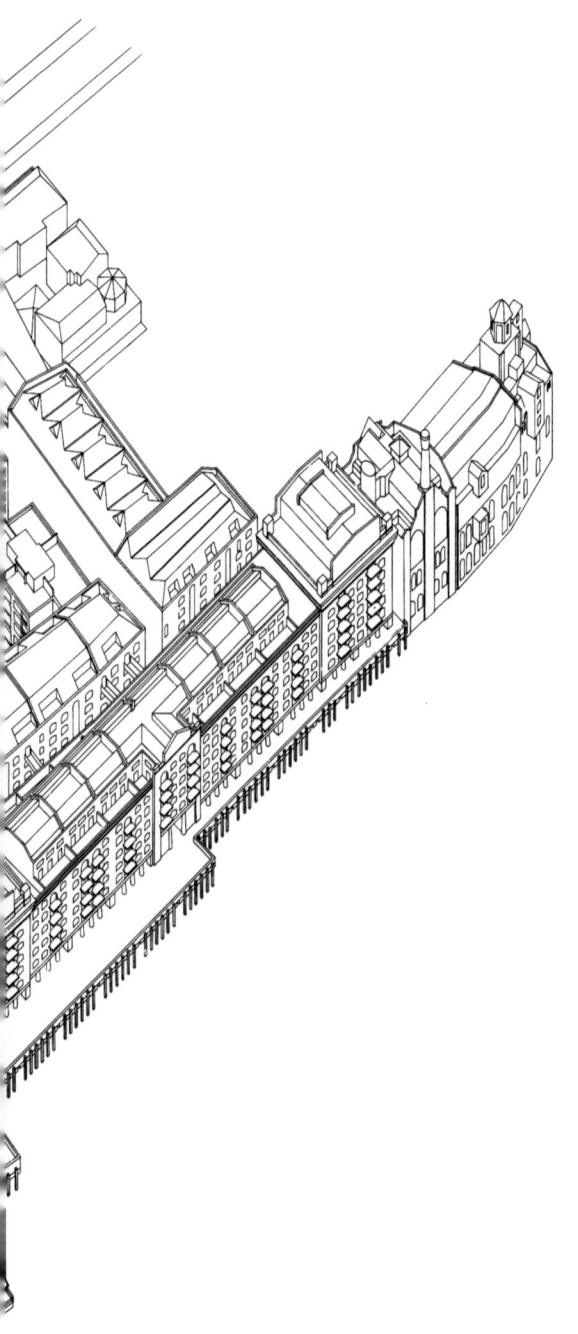

Conran Roche's original masterplan for the eleven-acre Butler's Wharf site. The large new block next to the Design Museum was commissioned by a software company as its headquarters, but was never built. The rest of the project was only partially implemented before the banks stepped in and took control

Terence identified a 1950s banana-ripening warehouse on Shad Thames as the Design Museum's first permanent home in 1986, and the nature of how difficult things had been previously is made clear in the correspondence between Southwark's planning department and the museum. In reply to the museum's request for guidance on an application for change of use for the building, Southwark wrote back: 'We are not the planning authority now that the London Docklands Development Corporation has taken over responsibility. But I must tell you that if we were we would not look favourably on a change of use, since this runs counter to our employment protection policies for the area.' Southwark's planners had already done their best to prevent the building of the Globe Theatre at Bankside for similar reasons. It was a policy based on the best of intentions but planners, like generals, have a way of fighting the battles of the next war with the tactics of the last one. After Bankside's power station became Tate Modern, Southwark's attitude changed dramatically.

Terence's strategy for the Shad Thames development was capital intensive. He spent heavily on the infrastructure of the area, creating an embankment and converting the riverside buildings before marketing them rather than selling off-plan. It placed an impossible burden on his cash flow, especially when the property market went into a downturn. His bankers refused to wait for better trading conditions and forced the site into administration in 1990. The bank sold the parcels of land that had not already been developed. But Terence was left in place to work on a string of riverside restaurants, and also bought the building on Shad Thames that Michael and Patty Hopkins had recently designed and built as a shop for David Mellor to sell his cutlery, and where he briefly lived with his wife, Fiona MacCarthy.

Julyan Wickham, the architect son of Terence's old friend Michael Wickham, designed and built a major part of it, Horselydown Square. Allies and Morrison and Piers Gough of CZWG designed other pieces, broadly following the Conran Roche masterplan with a mix of residential, restaurants and workspaces that maintained the urban grain of the area. It created a model that still looks impressive today, especially when set against the marching ranks of high-rise towers that now line much of the Thames.

[1] Paul Farley, 'Natural habitat: Sir Terence Conran in the hotseat', *Furniture News* (8 January 2020), www.furniturenews.net/interviews/articles/2020/01/1202541873-natural-habitat-sir-terence-conran-hotseat [Accessed 16 September 2021].

Design and culture

TERENCE CONRAN　MAKING MODERN BRITAIN

Terence had been much impressed by his visit, in 1946 as a schoolboy, to the *Britain Can Make It* exhibition at the otherwise empty Victoria and Albert Museum. Many of the most precious parts of the museum's collection had been evacuated in 1939: the ceramics had been packed up in boxes and moved to safety in a disused Piccadilly Line tunnel at the Aldwych Underground station; the rest of the collection was either at Montacute House in Somerset, or hidden in a quarry in Wiltshire. But before the collection returned to its home, the majority of the museum was given over to this lavishly spectacular exhibition, which was organised by the newly established Council for Industrial Design.

Britain Can Make It was partly an optimistic affirmation that a new and more modern Britain was in the process of emerging from the trauma of war. The exhibition was also a shop window for the export drive that would be required for Britain to be able to pay for that war. Given the cultural climate of the time, when the well-intentioned and the well-bred felt it was their duty to instruct the less fortunate in questions of taste, the exhibition contained a stern lesson in civic responsibilities aimed at teaching the public both the practical and the moral benefits of 'good' design.

Britain Can Make It was a prelude to the Festival of Britain in that it had a similar strategy of trying to make the message more palatable – a bit like spreading jam over dry bread. There were highly didactic displays produced by the Design Research Unit and by Max Fry and Jane Drew. Ernest Race's new BA chair, made from aluminium scrap salvaged from Spitfires, went on show alongside Wells Coates's Bakelite EKCO radio. There were room sets and interactive questionnaires.

For perhaps the first time, the British public had been introduced to the idea that the designer not only existed but might be a hero figure. Misha Black devised a display that was called How to Design and Make an Egg Cup. It included a giant plaster egg, and a machine stamping out thousands of functioning examples. In attempting to describe the significance of industrial design, Black began his exhibition with the following text:

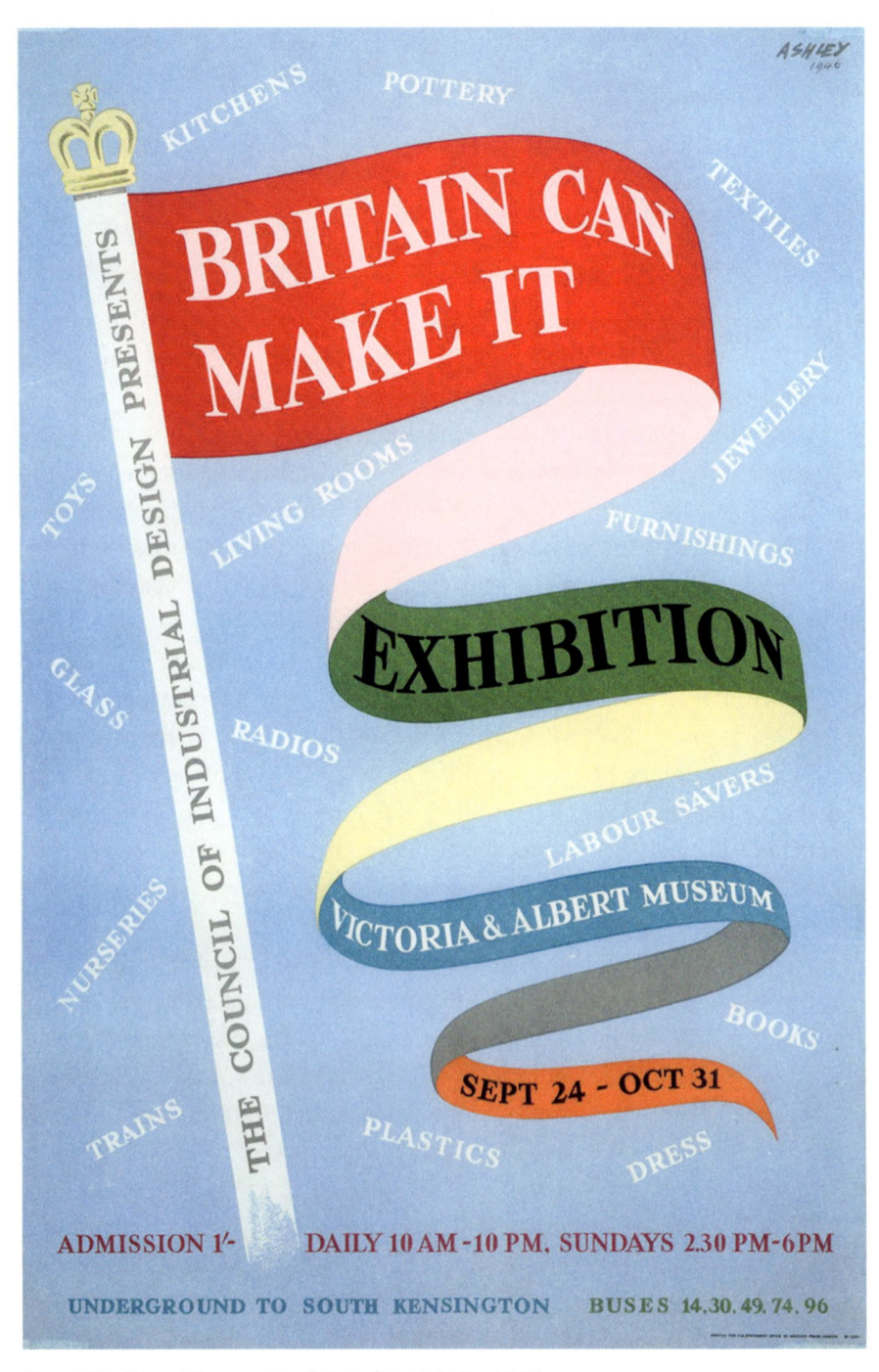

Almost 1.5 million visitors saw the *Britain Can Make It* exhibition

DESIGN AND CULTURE

Here is the Man
He solves all these questions
He decides what the eggcup shall look like
He is the Industrial Designer
He works with the Engineers, the
Factory Management – and is
influenced by what you want.

The exhibition was originally planned to run for just five weeks, from September to the end of October, but mile-long queues forced an extension to the end of the year. Eventually almost 1.5 million people paid to see the show.

Misha Black introduced industrial design to the public through the medium of egg-cup manufacturing

A space-saving kitchen by Max Fry and Jane Drew

For Terence, the exhibition was an eye-opener. It gave him an insight into the full range of what design might mean. It was also the start of his lifelong relationship with the V&A, and the beginning of his own ideas for what he might be able to do to influence both official policy and public understanding of design through the medium of a museum.

As a student, Terence kept coming back to the V&A's newly reopened galleries. Under Dora Batty's guidance, the Central School's textile designers were directed to spend time in the V&A's historic collections. There Terence acquired

The Council for Industrial Design used the exhibition to show the public the kind of products that they were encouraging industrialists to manufacture in the hope of improving the appeal of British products

a real affection for the sprawling museum that had been set up by Henry Cole and designed and built by the military engineer Captain Francis Fowke. As Terence became aware of the history of the V&A, he began to identify with the original vision of its founder Henry Cole, who saw the museum as a place to inspire and educate manufacturers and designers, and to help them put to use what they saw.

Following the triumph of the Great Exhibition, Cole, a man who was just as driven as Terence, and whose career had included magazine publishing, design and a ceramics business, set about reforming the national network of Government Schools of Design established after 1837. Cole argued that the schools had diverged from their founding principles, which he suggested were:

> *to provide for the architect, the upholsterer, the weaver, the printer, the potter and all manufacturers, artisans better-educated to originate and execute their respective wares, and to invest them with greater symmetry of form, with greater harmony of colour, and with greater fitness of decoration to render manufactures not less useful by ornamenting them, but more beautiful, and therefore more useful.*[1]

These goals were much the same as Cole's ambitions for the museum itself. He appeared to blame the students as much as their professors for the failure of the schools to do so.

> *Students did not exist sufficiently qualified by previous art education to enter them but had to be trained not merely to understand and practise*

DESIGN AND CULTURE

Henry Cole, responsible for the creation of the V&A, initially called it the Museum of Manufactures when it was based in Marlborough House

Cole included a section on what he called 'design on false principles'. It included this print, which Cole objected to for its super realism

the principles of design but to learn the very elements of drawing. Indeed, principles of design were hardly admitted to exist. Instead of being a school for teaching the principles and practice of applied art, circumstances had necessitated that they teach the basics of drawing and they were under the obligation of teaching little else than the mere ABC of art.[2]

In today's language, Cole was suggesting that the design schools were forced to concentrate too much on basic design skills, and not enough on applying design in the world. But these were not the same as the objectives followed by Cole's successors. The museum's focus, even before Cole's death in 1882, was shifting away from the practical towards the fine arts. And its acquisitions were less aimed at finding where design was going than celebrating where it had been. The V&A dispatched examples of Cole's own design work, produced under the pseudonym of Felix Summerly, from South Kensington to its satellite in Bethnal Green, and took on Raphael's Cartoons from the Royal Collection. It was a shift that could be understood as a reflection of British prejudices against utility and the ambition of a museum that was looking to build its own prestige.

As a museum curator, Cole believed in using objects to make a clear point. Before the move to South Kensington, Cole set up in Marlborough House on the Mall, where he showed what he regarded as the best of what designers could offer with items he had acquired from the Great Exhibition. He also staged an exhibition of what he called 'design on false principles' – gas lamps pretending to be candles,

Under Paul Reilly's leadership, the Design Council's black and white tags 'as selected for the Design Centre' were, consciously or not, following in Cole's path that started with his distrust of inappropriate ornament

textiles that were based on over-emphatically life-like representations of natural forms. It was a display that attracted mockery from Cole's acquaintance Charles Dickens, and Cole had the wit to confess that this morality tale of an exhibition was his most popular.

It was an expression of the continuing impulse in Britain to dictate on questions of taste, and to equate 'good' design with moral virtue. It was the same impulse that persuaded the Design Council to initiate its scheme to grant black-and-white triangular tags that attested to the virtue of items selected for the Council's index of approved products.

In much of the first half of the twentieth century the V&A's directors and curators were reluctant to acquire contemporary design for the museum's collection. It had become a museum of the decorative arts, unburdened by the embarrassment of utility, rather than of design. Despite Henry Cole's founding vision for the V&A as an institution concerned with modern manufacturing, it became for a while a place for the connoisseur of the exquisite rather than the contemporary.

Sir John Pope-Hennessy, its director in the 1970s, was the embodiment of this attitude. He was a scholar who knew a great deal about Italian Renaissance sculpture but had little interest in the products of twentieth-century industrial design. If such things were allowed into the V&A at all, it was through the increasingly marginalised travelling exhibitions of collections condescended to by the more academic keepers, while they pursued what was regarded as the more elevated study of artefacts untainted by concerns of modern commerce.

Mark Haworth-Booth, a photography curator at the V&A, recalls the day in 1972 when Reyner Banham's plans for an exhibition entitled *Invention and Design* were rejected by Pope-Hennessy.

> *We hoped that it would stimulate a broader appreciation of design. Banham briskly disposed of the idea of 20th-century design classics. The century, he declared, had only produced one design classic in its first three score years and ten – the Barcelona chair, by Mies van der Rohe. And that, he added, could have been made at any time in the last 2,000 years.*

> *Banham's proposal for the show involved a study of chairs, bicycles, radios, typewriters, telephones and kitchen appliances. All that was required was the approval of the V&A's director ... Sir John Pope-Hennessy listened to the proposal and then told us of a visit he had recently made to the Moderna Museet in Stockholm. There he had*

British visitors found the Milan Triennale exhibitions more sophisticated than anything they could see at home

Italian manufacturers rebuilding an economy destroyed by war used design to move up from low-cost copies of French and German originals

Sir Paul, later Lord Reilly, with the Duke of Edinburgh outside the Haymarket Design Centre. As director of the Design Council, Reilly was skilled at building establishment support for his campaigns. He was an early supporter of Terence, mentioning his name in an article in *Design* magazine as early as 1950. He was the first chair of the Conran Foundation, and provided the gravitas the Boilerhouse Project needed to be taken seriously by the government

*seen, he said, a marvellous exhibition about kitchen design. This would surely be a far more interesting subject. There was an appalled silence, into which I inserted the question, 'Yes, but how do you define what belongs in a kitchen?' The Pope's reply was unhesitating: 'I don't know, I never go in my kitchen.'*³

Terence had an early experience of more dynamic displays of contemporary design. He had been to see the Milan Triennale several times, most likely from as early as 1954 on one of his trips to collect an espresso machine or to buy furniture. The Triennale, based in a rationalist exhibition building designed by Mario Sironi in a park close to the Sforzesco Castle, displayed contemporary design from around the world using impressive display techniques.

The V&A was reluctant to show twentieth-century design, much as the pre-war Tate had neglected Picasso and Henry Moore. Meanwhile, the Museum of Modern Art in New York had acquired a Cisitalia sports car designed by Battista 'Pinin' Farina in 1951, which was also shown in an exhibition on car design in the same year. For Arthur Drexler, MoMA's curator, the automobile was 'hollow rolling sculpture'. The first time that the V&A showed a car was when Terence opened the Boilerhouse in 1981.

Terence began to think seriously about how he might be able to create an institution for Britain to spotlight contemporary design once Habitat was firmly established. It was a question that he discussed with Paul Reilly, later Lord Reilly, the cherubic director of the Design Council and son of Sir Charles Reilly, director of the Liverpool School of Architecture. Terence had cultivated Reilly for many years; he had presided over the opening ceremony not just of the Conran factory in Thetford, but also of the Conran contract showroom when it moved from Hanway Place to Tottenham Court Road in 1968.

For Reilly, who had worked for the Design Council and its predecessor, the Council of Industrial Design, for almost thirty years, it was necessarily a nuanced and somewhat political conversation. For Terence to talk about doing something new for design was to hint that there was something that both the Design Council and the V&A were failing to do. Reilly perhaps unwittingly found himself in the position of undermining the institution that he had devoted most of his career to building up.

After carrying out a review of the Design Council activities, the Thatcher government had decided that the Council's focus should no longer be the public, nor the design community, but it should instead limit its role to advising officials on how to address business. This was the beginning of a steady decline in the Council's visibility. What had once been a generously staffed and funded organisation, with its own monthly magazine, run as a non-departmental government body, closed its

Stephen Bayley established the Boilerhouse at the V&A, and then the Design Museum on its first site at Shad Thames, leaving within months of the opening in 1989

While the Tate and the Science Museum were reluctant to accept Bayley's plan for a gallery of industrial design, Roy Strong offered space for the Boilerhouse. The relationship was not an easy one, and came to an end after three years

Haymarket Design Centre to the public in 1994 after almost forty years, and was eventually converted into a private charity.

Reilly's own attitudes to design were certainly puritanical. In an echo of Henry Cole's gallery of design according to false principles, Reilly's Design Council took it upon itself to campaign against electric fires adorned by three-dimensional representations of burning logs, and electric toasters decorated with wheatsheaf graphics.

Rightly or wrongly, Reilly himself was a passionate advocate of good design in the moralising sense. There was a row over the Design Council's Design Centre shop on Haymarket, which stocked surreal teapots and cups with whimsical little legs by Christopher Strangeways. They did not accord with Reilly's view of what design should be about. But his successors lacked the same conviction and authority. As a result, the Design Council was losing the influence that it once had, and its black-and-white selection tags had come to be seen as something of a period piece. Its role would soon shift away from preaching to the public to advising business people who remained notably unconvinced.

Before Reilly stepped down as director in 1977, the Council had embarked on a publishing programme that took a wider view of the cultural significance of design. It published a monograph on Ernest Race, and commissioned Penny Sparke to write a companion volume on Ettore Sottsass.

Reilly had also seen *In Good Shape*, a proposal written by Stephen Bayley, a twenty-seven-year-old academic at the Open University, finally published as a book by the Design Council in 1979. It was a monochrome catalogue of uncontroversial modernist objects that ran from Peter Behrens's kettles designed for AEG to the Citroën DS 19. Reilly suggested that Terence meet Bayley and ask him to come up with a plan for what a museum of industrial design might entail.

When Bayley drew up his first proposal for a museum of industrial design, he had considered the idea of a brand-new building in Milton Keynes: the outcome

Art and Industry, the opening exhibition in the Boilerhouse at the V&A, 1982

of a conversation with Fred Lloyd Roche, who was still chief executive of the new town at the time. It was also where the Open University was located. Bayley's first academic job had been with the OU, working on its design programme. Reilly, however, suggested a museum in London as a venue. Bayley failed to make headway with Alan Bowness, the director of the Tate at the time, and later Neil Cossons at the Science Museum. Reilly suggested the V&A as its home which, with Roy Strong appointed as a new director in 1973, seemed a more promising venue than the other national museums.

In 1977, the V&A had closed its travelling exhibitions department, one of the few parts of the museum actively interested in the twentieth century, and it had a clear need to be seen to be doing something about design. Strong had built his early reputation with a flamboyant term as director of the National Portrait Gallery, and was prepared to listen to Conran and Bayley's approach.

He found a space in the basement for Conran to fund Bayley's idea. It was known as the Boilerhouse, because of what the space had once accommodated. The plan was for provocative temporary exhibitions that would attract headlines and focus public attention on the subject. Bayley's view was that contemporary art had lost touch with the public, and that its place in culture had been taken by design.

A bargain was struck that saw Terence give the V&A £700,000 for the museum to use as it saw fit. Terence also agreed to pay for the cost of fitting out the Boilerhouse, and to cover the bill for the exhibitions programme. In exchange, Terence became a V&A trustee and remained in the role until 1990, a few years after Strong had been replaced as the director by Elizabeth Esteve-Coll.

This was a time well before large-scale private donors had become common in British museums. It is safe to say that the response to the overtures from Terence was not immediately positive. Partly it was the subject matter: design was still seen as overtly commercial, and therefore not really an appropriate matter for a museum. There was also a certain level of anxiety about the prospect of ceding control of substantial areas of a museum to a project that came from outside. Museums prefer to formulate their own ideas about new developments, and then go out to find funders to realise them. Terence came to the V&A with Bayley's feasibility study and a chequebook to make it possible.

There were well-publicised tensions between Terence's team and the V&A from the beginning. Bayley had little interest in accommodating the views of the museum's curators, and the downside of the cuckoo-in-the-nest arrangement with the Boilerhouse quickly became apparent to its hosts. The V&A's visitors saw no difference between the Boilerhouse and all its other galleries. As far as they were concerned it was all the product of the same museum, whether it was the Great Bed of Ware or a Ford Sierra. When Bayley choose to explore Coca-Cola's branding history, the curators in the museum felt personally affronted. As they saw it, this was a vulgarisation of their scholarship. And there were other curatorial missteps. Bayley's exhibition *Taste* infuriated the architect Terry Farrell, who had loaned a model of his design for the breakfast television broadcaster TV-am, popularly known as Egg Cup House because of its postmodern flourishes and far-from-subtle iconography. Bayley's curatorial strategy was to place projects that met his criteria for good taste on plinths, and to put those which did not on dustbins. Farrell marched into the gallery and unilaterally repossessed his model.

It was rows like these that led to Strong's inevitable decision not to renew the Boilerhouse lease. In effect this meant that the V&A turned down Terence's offer to fund a modern wing, and it was the start of an increasingly rocky period for the V&A. Its Daniel Libeskind-designed Spiral extension was abandoned when it failed to get any lottery funding.

In retrospect, the Boilerhouse experiment has helped to transform the nature of the V&A, despite the pain that it caused at the time. In the forty years since then, the techniques of display and curating have been transformed. The idea of mixing film, sound and objects would once have been regarded as unthinkable. The V&A is still a place that shows its Raphael Cartoons, and where people come to see its extraordinary collections of ceramics and glass from every period of world history and from across the globe. But it has also learned how to explore popular culture in a way that very few of the world's museums of decorative arts have managed.

More recently, the V&A has taken an interest in Terence's own work. In 2021, it listed thirty-nine items in its collection that it describes as having been designed by Terence, as well as a similar number manufactured by Conran and Co., but designed by others. Almost all of them are from the earliest part of his career and relate either to his textiles, or to his work for the Midwinter Pottery. The V&A has a sample of his Tree Section print for Conran Fabrics from 1957, and the silk screen-print on linen known as Totem Leaf from the same year. It also holds a substantial archive donated by Habitat, as well as Paul Reilly's papers that relate to the establishment of the Design Museum.

The termination of the Boilerhouse lease led to rapid reassessment of Terence's plans: he was going to start a new museum of his own, and rather than build a department in an existing institution, Terence had a much better idea than Milton Keynes or the Tate as a location. He had seen an eleven-acre site of handsome, but redundant, warehouses at Butler's Wharf, just to the east of Tower Bridge on the south bank of the Thames. It would be a useful addition to

DESIGN AND CULTURE

In the whole of its history, the V&A had never displayed a car until the Boilerhouse opened in 1981

After Cole's design according to false principles, and the Design Council's black-and-white triangles, came the Boilerhouse's *Taste* exhibition

Terence's redevelopment plans for the area to have a cultural institution such as a design museum as an anchor attraction, much as department stores were once the anchors for shopping malls.

The run-up to the opening of the new museum, a converted banana-ripening warehouse built in the 1950s in Shad Thames, was particularly difficult for Terence. His marriage to Caroline was coming to an end. He walked away from Storehouse, and the Butler's Wharf development was forced into receivership when the Midland Bank called in its loans.

Bayley and Terence's relationship was also becoming strained. It became clear that building a new museum demanded more than good ideas. The Conran Foundation appointed Adrian Ellis, a former civil servant at the Treasury, as development director. He had a brief to shore up the gaps in Bayley's management and implementation skills.

Terence's architectural practice handled the conversion, which, with its flat roofs, white cement rendered walls and glass bricks, paid deliberate tribute to Walter Gropius' Bauhaus. Stanton Williams were responsible for the gallery interiors.

The Design Museum was opened by the prime minister, Margaret Thatcher, in 1989, with a spectacular firework display from a barge moored on the Thames, and a temporary lift breakdown that momentarily trapped Terence and the prime minister.

The opening exhibition was called *Culture and Commerce*, and it was designed by David Davies and Stuart Baron, a consultancy that had designed shops for the Next chain but had no previous experience of a cultural project. As a manifesto for the opening of a new institution it was confused, but it certainly represented a very different view of what design might be when compared with the opening exhibit at the Boilerhouse, which was called *Art and Industry*.

However, in comparison to the Boilerhouse, where visitors had to pay for an entrance ticket to the V&A but could gain admission to the exhibitions without separate charges, and which had the benefit of a guaranteed audience from the almost two million visitors who came each year to look at the rest of the V&A, the Design Museum in Shad Thames looked like poor value. The comparison was even more stark after 2001, when admission charges were abolished for national museums.

The Design Museum at Shad Thames had to fight for audiences and budgets. It had no choice but to charge for everything. Its ambitious early plans, which involved a rich public programme and even a short-lived ferry service to bring visitors from the Tower of London, were unsustainable. And to add to its problems, Bayley left the museum immediately after the opening.

A 1950s warehouse transformed into a tribute to the Bauhaus on the Thames

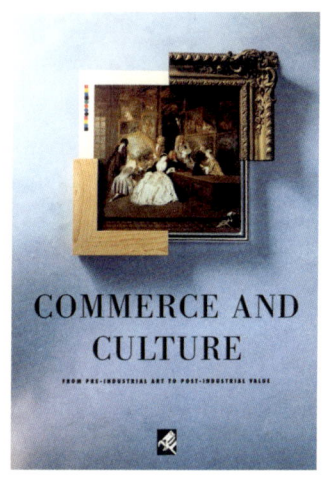

The opening exhibition at the Design Museum at Shad Thames

The next decade was difficult for the Design Museum. It had no regular public funding. It was attracting around 100,000 paying visitors every year, an impressive number for a hard-to-find location, but since this figure was smaller than when it had been in the V&A, it seemed a disappointment even if it was a much more committed audience. Unlike the publicly funded museums, the Design Museum had little in the way of a permanent collection to fall back on. Opting not to have a collection had been a deliberate decision when confronted with the three million or so objects in the V&A's collection.

Helen Rees, a member of the curatorial team, became the director on Bayley's departure. Three years later she was followed by Paul Thompson, who was director from 1992 until 2001, when he moved to New York to run the Cooper-Hewitt National Design Museum, a part of the Smithsonian Institution. In 2008, when Thompson was appointed as rector at London's Royal College of Art, Terence was the provost.

Rees and Thompson had the job of stabilising a modestly sized institution, and the museum emerged from its period of financial instability.

The museum moved on and appointed Alice Rawsthorn, a *Financial Times* journalist and a museum trustee at the time, as director in 2001. By this time James Dyson had become the museum's chairman. Terence admired Dyson's ability to succeed in business by inventing new and original products. Dyson's ever-growing fortune was also important. The Design Museum needed deep-pocketed supporters, in the manner of American museums where board membership brings with it a clearly stated obligation to donate every year.

Rawsthorn filled the galleries with quick-fire exhibitions, commissioned a new identity for the museum, and adjusted its content to recognise that design is a widening field, in which the digital and the intangible are increasingly important. There was more work by women, and a recognition that design is not only a question of functionalist problem-solving but can also be speculative and questioning.

These were not necessarily easy steps for Terence to follow, but he accepted them. More difficult was a personality clash between Dyson and Rawsthorn, who had no experience of working with a board of trustees as a director.

Dyson left after a majority of the trustees were reluctant to back his attempts to rein in Rawsthorn and her determination, as he saw it, to pursue a programme pitched more at the readers of *Wallpaper** magazine than the followers of Walter Gropius.

The last straw for Dyson was an exhibition about Constance Spry. According to Rawsthorn and its curator, Libby Sellers, this was an unusual opportunity to provide an insight into the way that popular tastes were shaped in the 1940s and 1950s, through the role of an interesting and unusual figure in that milieu. Dyson did not agree. With Conran's support, he demanded that Rawsthorn ensure the trustees had the chance to do more than rubber-stamp her programme and that she agree to an annual meeting to look at the museum's objectives and programmes. At the time, Terence was attempting to be conciliatory. 'We don't want to tell her what to do – the final decisions are hers, but we want to be able to discuss policies,' he told me in an article I wrote for *The Observer*.[4]

Design, said the most successful inventor of his generation, was about serious, technical things, not shallow styling. The museum should be about turbo-fan jet engines and body scanners, not football boots, frocks and hats – an emphasis that Dyson said was 'ruining the museum's reputation and betraying its purpose. It's become a style showcase, instead of upholding its mission to encourage serious design of the manufactured object,' he told *The Times*.[5]

At Dyson's suggestion, the museum staged an exhibition on Isambard Kingdom Brunel in 2000 and sold 27,299 tickets. It became clear that a Dyson approach was only possible with a generous level of financial support from either the government or sponsors. If the museum was going to pay for itself, it would need crowd-pleasers. So Rawsthorn gave shoe designer Manolo Blahnik a retrospective and sold 64,731 tickets. The figures speak for themselves.

Rawsthorn tried to make the museum less dependent on the financial support of the Conran Foundation, and succeeded in securing a substantial grant from the Department for Digital, Culture, Media and Sport for the education programme.

But the cost-cutting involved in this approach turned into a downward spiral, with the director attempting to carry out too many roles, and no budget for a full fund-raising or marketing team.

The Design Museum survived where many of the new institutions that opened around the turn of the millennium with the aid of large amounts of lottery funding did not. This is due not only to Terence's financial support but also its sense of purpose. In the early stages of the foundation of a new museum, a certain amount of turbulence is to be expected. Founders and directors inevitably clash about decisions.

In the most critical stages of the Design Museum's history, Terence was always generous enough to put the interests of the museum first. He didn't want Dyson to resign, and he hadn't wanted Rawsthorn to go. He had a lot of affection for Stephen Bayley, but in the end realised that the first director did not have the temperament to run a mature institution.

Terence knew that for the Design Museum to succeed in the way that he wanted it to, it could not be seen as his museum nor belong to any single director. It had to form a platform for a pluralistic approach.

After Dyson's departure, the trustees recruited Luqman Arnold, who ran the Abbey bank, to replace him. Arnold had attracted attention in the design world for commissioning the architect David Adjaye to work on a new retail concept for banking when he was running Abbey. Arnold had also impressed the City when he saved Abbey from the same fate that overtook Northern Rock, another former building society, by selling it to Santander.

Arnold took on the chairmanship of the Design Museum on the understanding that the museum would be embarking on a major reinvention. He donated a substantial amount to ensure that real work could start on this and, generously, Terence agreed to match the sum.

The existing building was too small to allow it to take on a deeper role, and to attract a larger audience. Furthermore, the lease was too short to justify the investment needed to rebuild it. Terence had been speculating optimistically about the possibility of taking over Battersea Power Station to do for design what the Tate had done at Bankside for contemporary art. Dyson talked about building a new Design Museum bridging the Exhibition Road in a symbolic connection of the Science Museum with the V&A.

More concretely, Nicholas Serota, director of the Tate, was ready to discuss the possibility of making land available on its site at Bankside. Initially, at least, the idea of becoming a neighbour to the most successful new contemporary art museum in the world, attracting five million visitors a year, certainly seemed attractive.

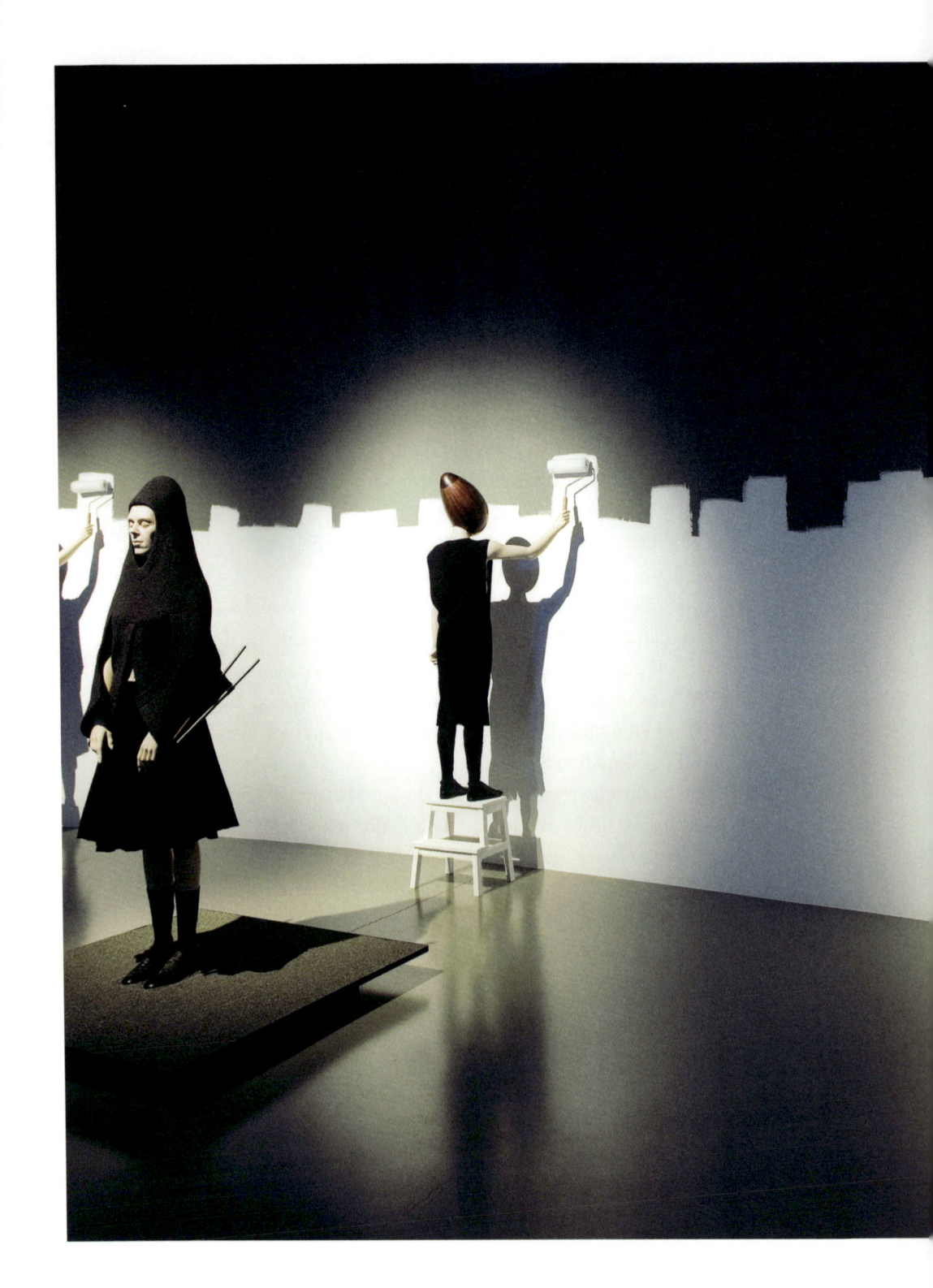

TERENCE CONRAN   MAKING MODERN BRITAIN

DESIGN AND CULTURE

The Design Museum's exhibition programme at Shad Thames mixed thematic exhibitions with retrospectives on major figures with a continuing relevance for the future, such as Hussein Chalayan (pictured here)

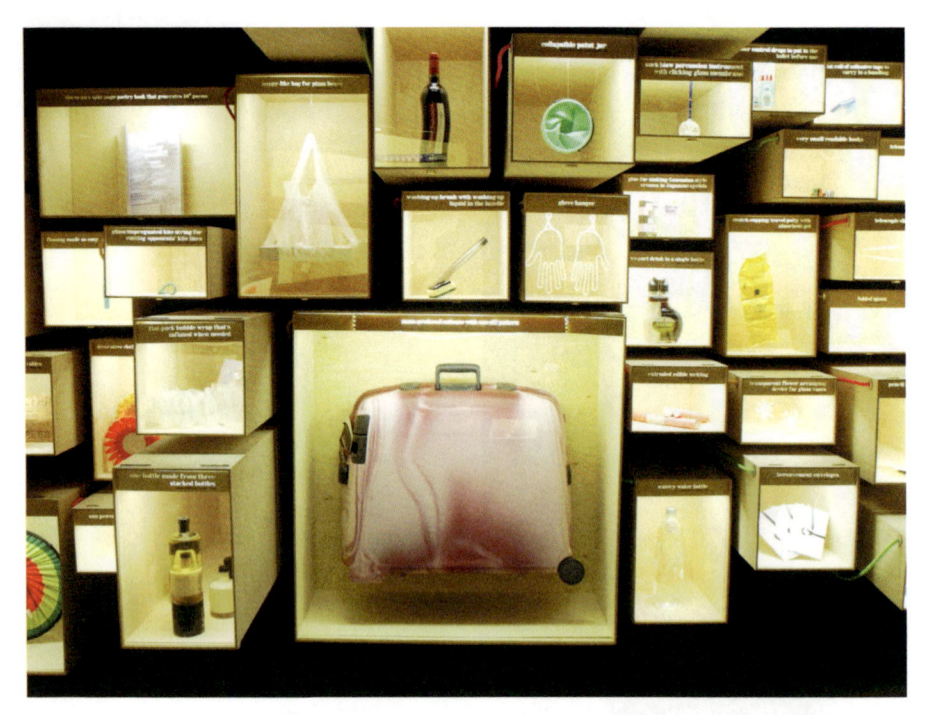

Each year, the Conran Foundation gave an individual a £25,000 budget to acquire items for the museum. They ranged from choices by Marc Newson to Thomas Heatherwick (pictured here)

Paul Smith's exhibition at the Design Museum in 2015 went on a world tour from Beijing to Tokyo

DESIGN AND CULTURE

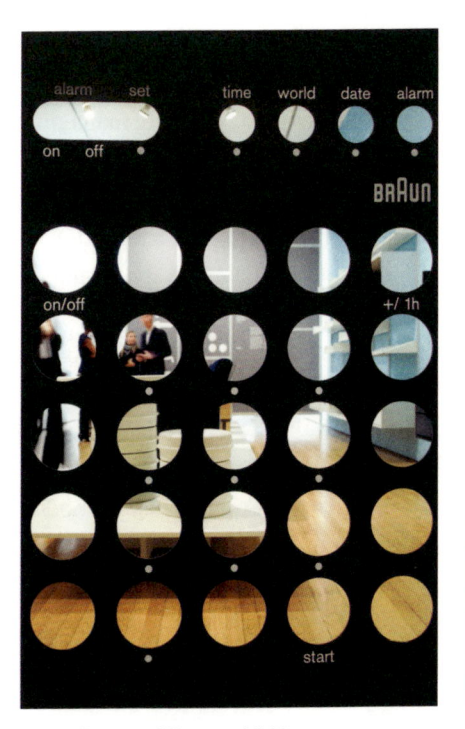

Dieter Rams and Braun exhibition

An evocation of Dieter Rams' home

Zaha Hadid had her first major UK exhibition at the Design Museum

As his first priority as the new chair, Arnold asked Rawsthorn to prepare a feasibility study for the project on the Tate site. He rejected the resulting document, and she left the museum shortly afterwards. Suzanna Taverne, formerly managing director of the British Museum, was brought in to advise the trustees on the steering of the museum until a new director was appointed.

I had just been offered the job of chief curator of architecture and design at the Museum of Modern Art in New York when Arnold called me in the spring of 2006 and took me to lunch to talk about the Design Museum. I explained that of course the prospect of the directorship would be interesting, but I was heading for America and it looked like I would be missing the opportunity. Over the next few days I had a series of calls from Terence, from Nicholas Serota and from other trustees suggesting that it would be a good idea for me to take the job.

When I had been appointed, I got a postcard from Phyllis Lambert, the founder of the Canadian Centre for Architecture in Montreal, and the woman who had persuaded her father Samuel Bronfman to commission Mies van der Rohe to design the Seagram Building in New York. 'Congratulations: perhaps you can make something of what I have always seen as a somewhat perfunctory institution.'

I started at the museum in August 2006, with a brief to steady the museum's operations on its existing site, to plan for the future and to maximise the museum's public impact by delivering a larger and more centrally located building. That involved mending fences with the previous chairman, but also developing a programme attractive enough to build up an audience. Alice Black, an MBA and former-banker-turned-museum-executive from the Imperial War Museum, joined me first as deputy director, and later alongside me as co-director.

It quickly became clear that the Tate site was not a real option. The land was on top of a working electricity substation and would need £25 million just to deal with it. Furthermore, Tate was planning to charge a market price for the land. Worse, the land was behind the Turbine Hall and had no riverside presence. We would be like a dinghy moored to an aircraft carrier. I broke the news to the trustees, and we agreed that we would need to start from scratch to look for a new site.

Arnold and I went to see Mark Jones, the director of the V&A, and he co-funded a feasibility study to see if the yard that now houses Amanda Levete's temporary exhibition gallery could work. It didn't seem large enough and, in any case, moving to the V&A would mean that the Design Museum would lose its independent identity.

We started to look at all the options, even walking across the mud-soaked construction site on the railway lands north of King's Cross.

Terence and I went to see Gordon Brown when he became prime minister. It was just after he had killed off Tony Blair's planned super-casino in Manchester, and he was clearly keen to find some good news for the northwest. Would we consider moving there? If so, government money might be available.

There had been too many museums that failed for making over-optimistic assumptions about audiences and income. A critical aspect of planning a new building was commissioning research to test the size of the audience for a larger-scale Design Museum. Without core public funding, it was essential to work with realistic figures on ticket, retail and events income. The figures for Manchester did not look good.

I met with the developers of Potters Fields, a site on the riverfront just south of Tower Bridge, who had planning permission for a housing scheme that depended on including 80,000 square feet of cultural space – just about big enough for our needs. We fenced with Tony Pidgley, the shrewd developer behind it, and drew up some plans on how a museum might be fitted into his project, but there was so much local opposition to his scheme that it did not seem worth it. Terence was getting impatient by this stage.

And then I had a conversation with David Prout, at that time chief planner at the Royal Borough of Kensington and Chelsea. Had the museum considered the former Commonwealth Institute as a potential site for its new home? There was a developer eager to build expensive apartments on part of the site he had recently bought, and the council was determined to use its powers under Section 106 of the Planning Act to bring the building back to life.

The development was a partnership between Elliott Bernerd and Ilchester Estates, the original freeholders of the land on which the Commonwealth Institute was built, fronted by Stuart Lipton. After a high-profile competition they had appointed Rem Koolhaas's architectural practice OMA to design the apartments.

For the developers, bringing the museum on board would unlock a problem. They could not start building without signing on a cultural institution with the resources to take on the Institute's exhibition building. And there were very few bona fide museums that needed the space and had the money required to fit it out, even if they got the lease for nothing. It also needed to be a museum that had a plan, which would convince both the Royal Borough of Kensington and Chelsea and English Heritage to withdraw their objections to the partial demolition of the listed building.

But this was not a building that came as a free gift, nor was Terence willing or able to underwrite the project. There was a prolonged negotiation in which the museum did its best to make the most of its position, securing a rent-free, 175-year lease with the option to extend it. And then the museum had to raise the money to fit out the new building.

Fundraising involved successful applications to the Heritage Lottery Fund and the Arts Council Lottery Fund. Terence gave the museum his head lease on Shad Thames, which was sold to Zaha Hadid. There were donations from many individuals, including all the trustees, as well as trusts and foundations. The museum was finally opened by the Duke of Edinburgh, who was given a tour of the building in November 2016. John Pawson's elegant transformation of a building that

Originally opened in 1962, the Commonwealth Institute – a listed building and modern monument – became the new Design Museum in 2016

was essentially a single space intended for a fixed display gave the museum two temporary galleries, as well as a permanent installation, and generous spaces for education and a library.

The new building afforded the museum three times the previous space. It also meant doubling its staff. The museum's chief curator Justin McGuirk's opening show was titled *Fear and Love*. It was a reflection of how the world's understanding of design has changed over the course of the thirty-five years since the Design Museum project was first formulated. It also reflected Terence's willingness to allow the museum the freedom to develop and respond to the continually changing nature of design, even though he had initiated it as an expression of his own views, rooted in the traditions of the arts and crafts in which he had been educated at Bryanston and the Central School. In recognition of his work, Terence was appointed by the Queen in 2017 to the Order of the Companions of Honour.

In the three years after it reopened on its new site, the Design Museum had more than two million visitors. For the last three years at Shad Thames, the total

John Pawson's conversion of the interior kept the soaring atrium and its hyperbolic parabola roof intact

was less than a quarter of that figure. It was named European Museum of the Year in 2018, and the conversion of the Grade II*-listed former Commonwealth Institute won a RIBA award. It has a dynamic online presence, with 4.2 million followers on Twitter. Peter Mandelson succeeded Luqman Arnold as chair. Tim Marlow was appointed as the museum's sixth director at the start of 2020. And during the COVID-19 pandemic the museum team secured £5 million from the

TERENCE CONRAN   MAKING MODERN BRITAIN

DESIGN AND CULTURE

As well as two temporary galleries, the Design Museum at Kensington opened a permanent display presenting design from the point of view of the maker and the user, as well as the designer

As part of *Designer Maker User*, the public was invited to nominate an object for display that had a special significance for them

Fear and Love: Reactions to a Complex World, the opening exhibition at Kensington in 2016

DESIGN AND CULTURE

Fashion has been a significant part of the museum's interests, with exhibitions on Hussein Chalayan, Christian Louboutin and Azzedine Alaïa (pictured here)

The *Ferrari: Under the Skin* exhibition conveyed how a car is designed, engineered and manufactured

government emergency support scheme, the largest contribution from the state in its history. The Design Museum emerged in better shape from lockdown than many of Britain's other museums.

At the time of writing, Marlow has opened the museum doors again and plenty of visitors are coming to see the exhibitions, including *Charlotte Perriand: The Modern Life*, a show Terence would have loved.

Terence was an engaged, active member of the museum's curatorial committee. He loved his involvement with the Design Ventura programme that challenged Britain's schoolchildren to take part in teams to compete to design products that would go on sale in the museum shop. He always came to see the new winners present their royalty cheque to the charity of their choice. He loved seeing the museum full of people.

The last time I saw him, we shared a white Burgundy in his study at Barton Court, looking out at the garden: 'Well,' he said, 'what's next at the museum?'

[1] Henry Cole, *Department of Practical Art: Elementary Drawing Schools, 1853, National Art Training School* (George E Eyre & William Spottiswoode for HM Stationery Office: London, 1853), 1-26.
[2] Ibid.
[3] Mark Haworth-Booth, 'Camera Lucida', *frieze*, 99 (6 May 2006), www.frieze.com/article/camera-lucida [Accessed 16 September 2021].
[4] Deyan Sudjic, 'How a flower arrangement caused fear and loathing', *The Guardian* (3 October 2004), www.theguardian.com/artanddesign/2004/oct/03/art3 [Accessed 16 September 2021].
[5] Jonathan Glancey, 'Dyson resigns seat at Design Museum', *The Guardian* (28 September 2004), www.theguardian.com/uk/2004/sep/28/arts.artsnews [Accessed 16 September 2021]

Epilogue

We have grown sceptical about understanding design as the result of a process that is based on the work of a single individual. To build a restaurant, create a retail business, or start and run a factory takes the efforts of many people. Likewise, to produce a chair, a shirt or a smartphone requires a wide range of skills and talents. A laptop demands, among other things, a software engineer to write code, a graphic designer, and a production manager to ensure that, for example, the keyboard is robust in use.

Yet those individuals rarely align spontaneously. They are persuaded or seduced or led into doing so by people with the unusual ability that is often called charisma. Terence had that quality. When he talked about a meal, or a room, or a house, he could add a word here or there – 'good French bread' – or place a plain, simple chair, just enough to turn something ordinary into something special. It was the way he said the words – the emphasis was just right, and he could make the humblest of meals sound delicious. It was something that he could do for those who worked for him, too, as much as for the many people that he wanted to attract into his shops or his restaurants.

It is an ability that he could, and did, put to work in many different ways: it helped him run a workshop of craftspeople in a Notting Hill Gate basement and create a leading design institution. To attempt to run an organisation as large as Storehouse, and to start as many projects as Terence did is not a task for a patient man. The other side of charisma is a temper that can be fierce.

Throughout his career, Terence always had a way of involving those he was close to in his work. Brenda designed his first catalogue. Shirley was the driving force in the setting up of Conran Fabrics, opening a base in Terence's studio in Cadogan Lane to run it after their first son, Sebastian, was born. Caroline was an essential part of the birth and development of Habitat. Vicki worked with him on the Boundary hotel and restaurant, in London's East End, and on the Conran Foundation. He relied on his children and grandchildren for insights into what generations younger than his own were thinking.

Like many successful people, Terence could have succeeded in a variety of different ways. He could have focused on pottery and textile design, or furniture

TERENCE CONRAN   MAKING MODERN BRITAIN

EPILOGUE

The impressive Conran Shop in Seoul which
opened at the beginning of 2019

Terence and Vicki Conran at their home in France, 2005

making. He had the appetite to try to do all of them, and more. He saw himself as a designer, even at Storehouse. And, in the sense that design is a way of exploring issues from multiple viewpoints at the same time – to explore how an object or a space will be used, how it will be made, and the form that it should take – he was right.

As a textile designer, he had a way with pattern. As a welder, he could use the most basic of techniques and materials to make a convincing chair. But these abilities reflect the aesthetic preoccupations of the 1950s, when he was just beginning. What Terence really excelled at was knowing what might be about to happen. He always felt sympathy for those designers who shared his enthusiasm for making: a characteristic that Tom Dixon, Thomas Heatherwick and Jony Ive – three entirely different designers – all share.

Terence also felt a certain sense of obligation to the public good. It is why he invested in building the Design Museum and devoted endless amounts of time to the Royal College of Art.

For the museum he was a generous benefactor, not only with time and money. Even more significant was his generosity in being prepared to trust the museum to grow and mature.

Finally, he was an optimist. He believed that there were better ways to do things, if only we could find them. He set an example in the way that he lived that many have tried to follow. He believed in people, and that if you gave them a reasonable choice, you could trust them to do the right thing.

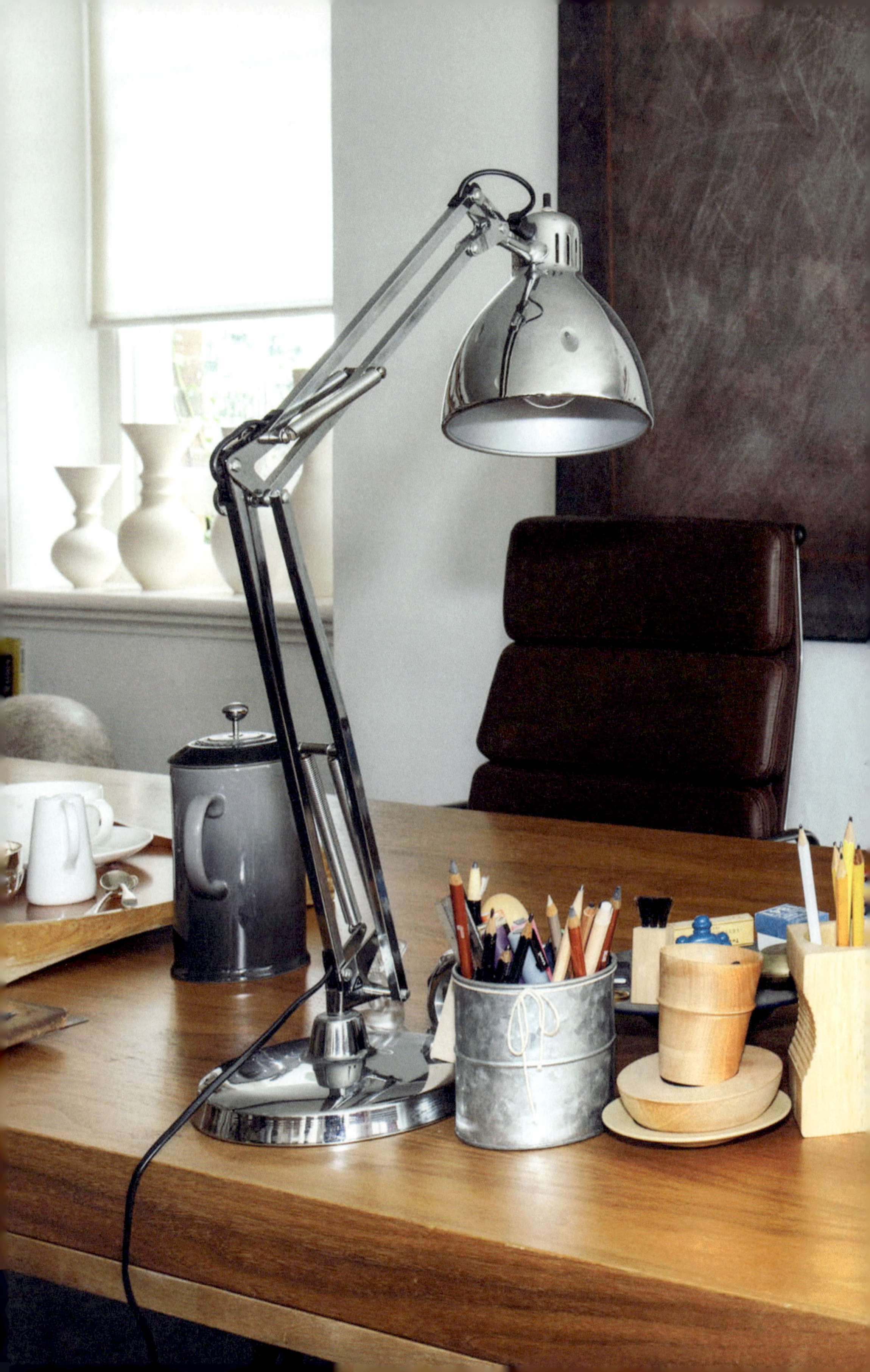

Cabinet
50

Index

A

A & F Parkes and Co. 96
Abbey National 211
Adams, Ansel 134
Adjaye, David 211
Ahrends, Burton and Koralek 29, 43, 53
Alaïa, Azzedine 223
Alcazar, Paris 141
Allies and Morrison 190
Almeida 141
Ambassador, The (magazine) 63, 69, 134
Amies, Hardy 68-9
Anderson, Laurie 59
Andrews, Colman 124
Apicella, Enzo 167
Aragon, Louis 89
Architectural Review (magazine) 49-50, 84, 87, 90, 91, 110, 127
Arcon 76, 77
Arnold, Luqman 211-16
Art and Industry exhibition 204, 208
Art Workers' Guild 36, 37
Arts and Architecture (magazine) 76
Arts Council 59, 74
Arts and Crafts 23, 37, 175-6
Ascher, Zikmund (Zika) 40, 134
Ashley, Bernard 107, 134
Ashley, Laura 107
Attlee, Clement 28, 65
Attwood, Martin 59
Austin, Frank 80
Ayer, AJ 129

B

Bacon, Francis 179
Baden Powell, Robert 30, 31
Baker, Josephine 118
Banham, Reyner 49, 199-201
Barber, Chris 153
Baron, Stuart 208
Barry, Gerald 73, 74, 84
Bartlett School 65
Barton Court residence 7, 9, 13, 15, 45, 45, 89, 224, 230
Batty, Dora 34-6, 63, 195
Bauhaus 37-8, 65, 91, 127, 148, 208, 209
Baxter, Walter 124
Bayer, Herbert 127
Bayley, Stephen 20, 202, 203-6, 208-9, 211
Bazaar 108, 145
Beazley, Michael 156
Becker, Dorothee 168

Behrens, Peter 203
Benchmark 9-13, 15, 16, 124, 140, 184
Benlox 181
Bennett, Alan 128, 129-31
Bernerd, Elliott 217
Bertoia 161, 169, 170
Bérard, Christian 120
Biba 145
Bibendum 136, 140-2
Birdsall, Derek 153
Black, Alice 216
Black, Misha 74-5, 76-7, 105, 193-5
Blackburn, Cynthia 87-8
Blahnik, Manolo 210
Blair, Tony 19, 138, 217
Blake, Peter 60
Blake, William 32
Blazer 18, 184
Bluebird 141-2
Blueprint (magazine) 19, 183
Blueprint Café 137, 140-1
Boilerhouse Project 201-4, 205-8
Bootes-Johns, Dudley 148
Boundary restaurant 142, 227
Bowness, Alan 205
Boxer, Mark, 'Life and Times in NW1' 128, 129
Boxgrove boarding school 26
Bradbery, Ian 93, 134, 153
Brancusi, Constantin 44, 73
Braun 147, 153, 159, 170, 215
Breuer, Marcel 53, 163
Brewer, Cecil 176
Britain Can Make It exhibition (1946) 65, 82, 105, 193-5
British Film Institute (BFI) 74
British Home Stores (BHS) 18, 175, 179-81, 183-4
British Library 49
British Museum 36
British Railways 105
Bronfman, Samuel 216
Brown, Gordon 217
Brumwell, Marcus 49, 105
Brunel, Isambard Kingdom 210
Bryanston 23, 27-33, 52, 68, 219
Bugatti collection 9, 12
Bunsen Street workshop 46
Burden, Jane 36
Burges, William 30
Burton, Richard 29, 44, 53, 55

Burton Group 152, 170, 180
Butler, Reg 80
Butler's Wharf 18, 59, 140, 178, 184, 185, 189, 190, 206-8
Buzz 177

C

C 7500 exhibition 59
Cadogan Lane studio 106-7, 114, 227
Café Boulevard 71
Calder, Alexander 40
Campaign for Nuclear Disarmament (CND) 96
Campus furniture 152-3, 160
Cantina del Ponte 137, 140
Cardew, Michael 32
Carnaby Street 36
Caro, Anthony 53, 55, 59
table piece 13, 16
Cassidy, Denis 181
Casson, Hugh 73-6, 82-4, 97, 101, 134
Central School of Arts and Crafts 13, 17, 19, 24, 34-49, 52, 63, 69, 96, 99, 153, 195, 219
Chalayan, Hussein 213, 223
Chandigarh, Punjab 64, 65
Chanterelle, The 124-5
Chippendale, Thomas 157
Chop House 137, 140
Chopping, Richard 'Dickie' 179
Chow, Michael 167
Churchill, Winston 73-4
Citterio, Antonio 183
City of London 175, 211
Clark, Kenneth 74
Clegg, Tony 179
Clendinning, Max 55
Cliff, Stafford 20, 164
Clinton, Bill 19, 138
Clinton, Hillary 138
Clive-Smith, Virginia 146
Coade, Thorold 29-30
Coates, Wells 82, 134, 193
Cock Yard, Camberwell 107
Cocteau, Jean 120
Cole, Henry 195-9, 203, 207
Colombo, Joe 159, 169
Commerce and Culture exhibition 208, 209
Commonwealth Institute 92, 217, 218, 219
Conran, Bernard Hamilton 25
Conran (née Herbert), Caroline 19, 55, 140, 148-9, 154, 157, 169, 177, 178, 208, 227

Conran (née Sloper), Charlotte Orby 25
Conran (née Halstead), Christina 13, 23-6, 27-8, 33-4, 36
Conran, Evelyn 25
Conran, Jasper 137, 179
Conran, Lewis Charles 25
Conran, Ned 148
Conran, Priscilla 13, 23, 24, 34, 127, 134, 183
Conran, Rupert 23, 24, 25-8, 33-4
Conran, Sam 33
Conran, Sebastian Orby 19, 25, 137, 179, 180, 227
Conran (née Pearce), Shirley 17, 36, 103, 107, 127-8, 131, 134-7, 140, 227
Conran, Sophie 148
Conran, Terence Orby
birth 23
books
Printed Textile Design 36, 84, 133, 134-7
The House Book 82, 156, 157, 166, 167
The Kitchen Book 166, 167
childhood 23-33
and collecting 7-9, 13, 141
death 7
and design 9, 37-8, 142, 230
education 13, 17, 23-49, 63, 219
eightieth birthday 16, 20
entrepreneurial streak 17-18, 23, 27
eye injury 27, 36
furniture 46, 50, 52, 91-3, 106, 111-13, 121, 127, 130, 145-72, 175-7, 230
C4 chair 106
C20 chair 106
S1 cabinet 93, 153
storage system 93, 94-5
table at the ICA 47, 50
and interior design 26, 124-7
knighthood 18, 178
and making 9, 13, 27, 32-3, 34, 46, 230
office 8, 11, 13, 175, 177, 179, 182, 183-4
optimism 230
politics 18
pottery 32-3, 34
restaurants 17, 18, 19, 24, 55, 57, 87, 119-27, 136-9, 140-2
and social class 24-5
and textile design 17, 34-6, 38-41, 69, 96, 99, 121, 131, 134-7, 206, 230
Chequers 63, 96, 97, 101
woodworking tools 13, 16
Conran, Tom 148
Conran (née Davis), Vicki (Terence's fourth wife) 33, 141, 227, 230

INDEX

Conran Associates 152, 178, 184
Conran and Co. 23, 25, 26, 87, 102, 107, 112, 148, 206
Conran Contracts 113
Conran Design Group 106, 107, 108, 110, 111, 152
Summa range 114, 153-4, 155
Conran Design Studio 111
Conran Fabrics 103, 134, 227
Totem Leaf print 206
Tree Section print 206
Conran Foundation 73, 201, 208, 210, 214, 227
Conran Group 125
Conran Octopus 156, 184
Conran and Partners 124
Conran Roche 107, 142, 187, 189
Conran Shop 125, 136, 140, 141, 170, 171, 175, 184, 229
Conran Studio 55, 185
Conservatives 69, 73-4, 179
Cooke, Cecil 82-3
Copp, Bruce 19
Cornish Crafts Association 19
Cossons, Neil 205
Costello, Elvis 148
Council for Industrial Design, The 70-1, 73-4, 77, 79-80, 82-3, 193, 196, 202
Courtauld Institute 49
Covent Garden 13, 55-9, 152, 187
Covid-19 pandemic 219
Craddock, Fanny 119
Crosby, Theo 52, 63
Crown Estate 19
Cunard 70
Cunard, Nancy 44, 89
Currie, Katie 148
CZWG 190

D
D&D 142
Dalham 114, 154, 168-9
Dalton System 29
Dartington Hall 29, 30
Davey, Geoff 183
David, Marquess of Queensberry 127, 179
David, Elizabeth 118, 124, 137, 166, 167-8
David, Sylvette 50, 88
David Whitehead Ltd 63, 69, 96, 97, 99, 101, 103
Davies, David 208
Davies, George 178
Davison, Brenda 71, 87, 88, 89, 153, 227
Day, Lucienne 63, 134

Day, Robin 80, 81, 113, 134
Debenhams 19, 148-9, 179-80, 183
Degus, Dick 76
Del Renzio, Toni 52
Den Permanente 145
Dench, Judi 119
Denny, Robyn 55, 60
Derain, André 40
Design Council 73, 198, 199, 201, 202-3, 207
Design Museum 18-20, 68, 92, 137, 206, 214, 230
contemporary site, Kensington 211-24
Shad Thames site 20, 44, 45, 73, 140, 184, 186, 190, 202, 206-11, 213, 218-19
Design Research store 145
Design Research Unit (DRU) 49, 74, 105, 193
Design Ventura programme 224
Designer Maker User exhibition 222
Dickens, Charles 199
Dixon, Tom 230
Docker Brothers 26, 27
Docklands, London 18, 172, 187-90
Dome (now the O2 Arena) 20
Domus (magazine) 76
Donegan, Lonnie 153
Donne Place, Chelsea 107
Donovan, Terence 145-6, 148, 151
Dover Street 49-50
Drew, Jane 49, 64, 65, 66, 68-9, 77, 193, 195
Drexler, Arthur 201
DSR fibreglass chair 53
Dufferin, Sheridan 53-4
Dukes, Ashley 92
Dury, Ian 148
duvets 168, 168
Dworkin, David 183
Dyson, James 209-11

E
Eames 145, 159, 161, 170, 171
Eames, Charles 53, 65, 76, 131, 170
Eames, Ray 53, 65, 131, 170
East End 36, 46, 49, 52, 53, 113-14, 227
Eckersley, Tom 134
Edelman, Asher 181
Edinburgh Weavers 63
Ehrenzweig, Anton 38, 39, 40
Electricity Board 105
Elizabeth II 139, 178

237

Elliot, Freda 41
Eliot, TS 74, 89
Ellis, Adrian 208
Emberton, Joseph 91
Envis, Jenny 26
Esher 23
Esteve-Coll, Elizabeth 205

F
Falklands War 18
Farina, Battista 'Pinin' 201
Farr, Michael 68
Farrell, Terry 206
Fear and Love exhibition 218-19, 222
Ferrari: Under the Skin exhibition 223
Festival of Britain 1951 18, 49, 53, 72, 73-84, 87, 105, 154, 193
  Countryside pavilion 77
  Dome of Discovery 75, 77, 82
  Homes and Gardens pavilion 78, 79-83
  Lion and Unicorn pavilion 152
  Natural Scene and Country pavilion 79, 82
  Pattern Group 76-7, 137
  Skylon 75, 76
  Transport pavilion 76, 77
  Festival Hall 74, 75
Fitch, Rodney 106-10, 152
Fitch and Co. 152
Fitzroy Street 17, 50-2
Fnac 183
Ford, Sydney 83
Foster, Norman 187
Fowke, Captain Francis 196
France 20, 55, 73, 88-9, 142, 164-7, 172, 184
Frayn, Michael 83
Frears, Stephen 128-9
Frederick Gibberd and Partners 106
Freud, Lucian 29, 31
Freud, Sigmund 9
Froshaug, Anthony 52
Fry, Max 49, 64, 65, 68, 77, 193, 195
Fulcher, Colin (Barney Bubbles) 146-8
Fulham Road 19, 145, 149, 151, 170, 175, 183

G
Gabo, Naum 105
Gallery One, Soho 41, 53
Galvin, Chris 125, 141
Games, Abram 72, 83
Garage gallery 13, 16, 55, 58-9, 187

Gardner, James 74, 76
Garland, Ken 96
Gentleman, David 129
Giacometti, Alberto 44, 45
Gibson, Alexander 77
Gibson, Natalie 103
Gielgud, John 74
Gill, Eric 30, 34, 38
Gillette 106, 107
Girard, Alexander 134, 145
Gloucester Crescent 128-9
Gloucester Place studio 65
Glynn-Smith, Juliet 154
Goldfinger, Erno 83
Goldstein, Sasha 36
Goodden, Robert 76, 152
Goodden, Wyndham 19
Gough, Piers 190
Government Schools of Design 196-8
Gray, Milner 105, 134
Gray, Rose 140
Great Eastern Hotel 141
Great Exhibition 1851 73, 75, 196, 198
Greater London Council (GLC) 55-8
Green, Philip 175
Greene, Alexander Plunkett 107
Greenwich Village 58
Gregory, Oliver 55, 110, 148
Groag, Jacqueline 68, 134
Gropius, Walter 37, 64, 65, 208, 210
Growth and Form exhibition (1951) 50
Guastavino 141, 142
Guérard, Michael 148
Guest, Helen 157
Guggenheim, Peggy 44, 73
Guinness 58, 181, 184
gum copal 23, 25
gun-making 34
Gunewardena, Des 142

H
Habitat 7, 18, 19, 20, 29, 82, 89, 110-11, 113, 129, 145-72, 151, 154, 175, 177-84, 181, 201, 206
  catalogues 19-20, 23, 55, 59-60, 153-9, 160-71, 183
  chicken brick 33
  cooks calendars 169
  expansion 149, 152
  floatation 178, 180
  launch 108, 145, 146, 149, 151, 170, 227
  and price point 170-1
  prints 59-60

INDEX

Habitat warehouse, Wallingford 29, 43, 44, 152
Hadid, Zaha 215, 218
Halpern, Ralph 19, 180
Hamilton, Richard 29, 41, 44, 50, 52, 127, 159
Growth and Form 48
Hamlyn, Paul 140, 156, 157, 181, 183
Hammer Prints, Thorpe-le-Soken 53
Hancock, Tom 152
Handley-Read, Charles 30, 34
Hanway Place 107-10, 114, 146, 152, 202
Hart Dyke, Lady 83
Harveys of Bristol 110, 111
Havinden, Ashley 63
Hawkwind 148
Haworth Fabrics 134
Haworth-Booth, Mark 199-201
Haymarket Design Centre 198, 201, 203
Heal, Oliver 177
Heal, Sir Ambrose 175-6
Heal's 18, 23, 149, 175-7, 179-80, 184
Heal's Building 17, 175-6, 179, 182, 183, 184
Heath, Adrian 29, 50-2
Heath, Edward 18
Heatherwick, Thomas 45, 214, 230
Heathrow airport 106
Henderson, Brian 149, 157
Henderson, Elizabeth 149
Henderson, Fergus 149
Henderson, Nigel 29, 41, 46-9, 52-3, 89-92, 148
Man in Bunsen Street 47
Parallel of Life and Art 48, 50
self-portrait 51
Henderson, Wyn 41-4
Henrion, FHK 77, 79, 82, 92
Hepworth, Barbara 63, 80, 177-8
Heseltine, Michael 107, 131, 187
Highfield prep school 26, 27
Hille 80, 113-14
Hilton, Roger 30, 52
Hippisley-Coxe, AD 83
Hobbs, Keith 55, 141
Hockney, David 53, 55, 57, 59, 60
Hodgkin, Howard 29, 30, 31, 55, 177
Hoffman, Josef 68
Holland, James 75, 76
Holton, Gerald 96
Hopkins, Michael 185, 190
Hopkins, Patty 185, 190
Hopkins, Simon 140

Hopkinson 141
Horrocks 63
Hotel Leofric 106
House and Garden (magazine) 87, 89, 97, 110, 131, 148, 183
Hulanicki, Barbara 145
Hunstanton School 53
Hunt, Tony 152

I

Ideas and Objects for the Home exhibition 1952 91
IKEA 157, 172
Ilchester Estates 217
Illums Bolighus 145
Independent Group 49, 52
India 25, 28, 65, 113
Institute of Contemporary Arts (ICA) 41, 48, 49-50, 52, 65, 69, 88, 124-5, 127
IRA bombings, London 18
Ismay, General Lord 74
Italy 44, 46, 49, 93, 113, 163, 167, 171, 199, 200
Ive, Jony 230

Jack Lenor Larsen textiles 113
Jacobs, Jane 58
Jacobsen, Bernie 60
Jacobsen Conran Ltd 60
Jacques, Hattie 119
Jaeger 70
James, Hillary 119, 134
Japan 20, 184
Jarman, Sonja 148
Jeffreys, Jeffrey Graham 29
Jellicoe, Geoffrey 70
Jellinek, Toby 50, 88, 89
Johnson, Philip 92
Johnston, Edward 34, 38
Johnstone, William 37-8, 41
Jones, Alan 142
Jones, Mark 216
Juda, Elsbeth 63, 69, 134
Juda, Hans 63, 69, 134
Julien, Michael 184
Justerini and Brooks 167

K

Kamprad, Ingmar 172
Kar, Ida 41
Kartell 113, 169
Karuselli 169
Kasmin (John Kaye) 41, 53-5, 57, 59
Katz, Bronek 78, 79

Kendall 178
Kensington 23
Kinsman, Lisa 169
Kinsman, Rodney 167
Kissin, Joel 141-2
kitchenware 166, 167-8
Knoll, Florence 113, 145
Kodatrace 40-1
Koolhaas, Rem 217
Korean war 73, 87
Krauss, Amy 32
Kroll, Natasha 91, 145
Kukkapuro, Yrjö 169-70

L
La Méditerranée 120, 129, 141
Labour governments 28, 69, 73-4
Lambert, Phyllis 216
Lane, Charles 27
Lane, Julia 177
LAR armchair 53
Lasdun, Denys 65
Le Corbusier 49, 64, 65, 71
Le Matelot restaurant 119, 134
Le Pont de la Tour 19, 137-8, 140-2
Leach, Bernard 32
Lee, Belinda 97, 102
Lee, Jeremy 141
Lee, Laurie 83
Left Bank, Paris 52
Leigh, Vivienne 125
Leith, Prue 167
Lennon, Dennis 46, 49, 63-5, 66, 68-71, 76-7, 84, 87, 92
Lethaby, William 34, 36-7
Levete, Amanda 216
Lewis, Wyndham 30
Leyland 108
Libby, Maurice 148
Libeskind, Daniel 206
Lightbown Aspinall 104
lighting 161, 169
Lippard, Lucy 59
Lipton, Stuart 217
Loewi, David 142
Logan, Andrew 187
Logue, Christopher 129
London County Council 36, 75, 113-14
London Docklands Development Corporation (LDDC) 187-90
London Steak Houses 70
London Transport 34, 35
London Underground 34, 38
Loos, Adolf 37

Lotte Department Store 229
Louboutin, Christian 223
Lucas-Tooth, Lady 83
Lupton, Tom 152
Lupton Morton 147, 152-3, 160
Lutyens restaurant 142
Lyons' Corner House restaurants 70, 118
Lyttelton, Patricia 121

M
MacCarthy, Fiona 30, 32, 190
MacMallum, Ian 50, 91-2
Magistretti, Vico 113, 153-4, 163, 172
Makepeace, John 13
Manasseh, Leonard 76
Mandelson, Peter 219
Mankowitz, Wolf 93
Manson, James 71-3
Marimekko 113, 145, 171
Marlow, Tim 219-24
Martin, Leslie 75
Marx, Enid 63
Maschler, Fay 167
Matisse, Henri 17, 40-1, 134
Matthew, Robert 75
Maufe, Sir Edward 176
Maufe, Prudence 176
Maurer, Ingo 168, 169
Mayor Gallery 13, 41-4
McAlpine, Alistair 178-9
McDouall, Robin 124
McGuirk, Justin 218
Mellor, David 55, 185, 190
Melly, George 129
Mercury theatre workshop, Notting Hill 92-3, 107, 111, 227
Metropolitan Museum of Art 87
Mezzo, Soho 142
Michelin building 136, 145, 183
Michelotti, Giovanni 108
Middle Earth club 58
Midwinter, Roy 96-103, 206
Mignet, Henri, Pou de Ciel 91
Miller, Jonathan 129
Milton Keynes 113, 184, 187, 203, 206
Ministry of Food 117
Mistry, Dhruva 141
Mitchell, Peter Todd 134
Mlinaric, David 71
modernism 37, 59, 65
Modigliani 176
Modus wallpaper 103, 104
Moholy-Nagy, László 91, 134
Moholy-Nagy, Lucia 134

INDEX

Moore, Henry 40, 71-3, 92, 201
Morgan Grenfell 149, 179, 181
Moro, Peter 75
Morris, May 36
Morris, William 36, 37, 38
Morse-Brown, Mr 83
Morton, Alastair 63
Morton, John 152
Moser, Claus 129
Mosscrop, Stuart 187
Mothercare 18, 149, 177-81, 184
Mountleigh 179, 180-1
Moya 75, 76
Murray, John 63, 69
Museum of Modern Art (MoMA) 49, 201, 216
Musgrave, Victor 41, 53

N

Neal, AS 50
Neal Street 152, 175
Neal Street Restaurant 54, 55, 57, 140, 141, 169
Nelson, George 145
New London Gallery 53
New Millennium Experience Company 19-20
New Towns 113
New York 49, 58, 87, 141-2, 149, 201, 209, 216
Newman, Barnett 55
Newson, Marc 214
Newton, Den 87, 88, 89, 90
Next 177, 178
Nicholson, Ben 17, 52, 63
Nimbus (magazine) 88
Noland, Kenneth 53, 55
North End Road, Fulham 107
nuclear weapons 71

O

Old Shepherd's Farm, Liphook 26
O'Leary, Eric 92-3, 107
Olivetti 137-40, 157, 183
OMA 217
O'Rorke, Brian 79, 82
Orrery restaurants 24, 87, 119, 122-3, 125-7, 140-1
Orwell, George 128
Ox on the Roof, The 118-19, 127
Oz (magazine) 146

P

P&O 105, 187, 190
Pamuk, Orhan 9

Paolozzi, Eduardo 13-17, 29, 39, 41-53, 84, 88, 118, 140, 148
Bunk lecture 50
Kalasan 43, 44-5
Parallel of Life and Art 48, 50
Suwasa 43, 44-5
table at the ICA 47, 50
terracotta tile 13, 16, 92-3
textiles 46, 70
Head of Invention 44, 45
Trishula 43, 44-5
Parallel of Art and Nature exhibition 124-5
Paris 44, 49, 52, 120, 129, 141
Partas brassière showroom 71
Pasmore, Victor 17, 52
Pawson, John 218
Penrose, Roland 49
Pentagram 63, 105
Peters, Michael 106
Pevsner, Nikolaus 37
Philip, Duke of Edinburgh 201, 218
Picabia, Francis 118
Picasso, Pablo 40, 50, 71, 88, 89, 176, 201
Piccadilly Arcade showroom 52, 93, 97, 106, 107
Pick, Frank 38
Pidgley, Tony 217
Piper, John, *The Englishman's Home* 78
Piretti, Giancarlo 157, 163
Pleydell-Bouverie, Katherine 32
Plunket Greene, Alexander 26, 107-8
Pollock, Phillip 148, 149
Ponti, Gio 76, 131
Pop art 50
Pope-Hennessy, Sir John 199-201
Portman, second Viscount 28
Portman family 29
posters 34, 77, 79, 134, 157-9, 160
Postgate, Raymond 118
Potter, Don 30, 31, 32, 45
Potters Fields 217
pottery 96-103
Pound, Ezra 89
Powell 75
Practical Equipment Ltd (PEL) 53
Princess flying boat 77-9
Prout, David 217

Q

QE2 (liner) 70
Quaglino's 139, 140-2
Quant, Mary 26, 107, 108, 109, 145
Knightsbridge shop 18

241

Queen magazine 131, 148
Queensberry, David 103

R
Race, Ernest 80, 193, 203
Rambert, Marie 92
Rams, Dieter 147, 159, 215
Raphael 198, 206
rationing 27, 28, 36, 40, 45, 80, 92, 117-18
Rawsthorn, Alice 209-16
rayon 65
Rayon and Design (magazine) 68-9
Rayon Design Centre 63, 65-8, 69, 76-7, 134
Read, Herbert 49, 105
Rees, Helen 209
Regent's Park Terrace residence 127-34, 137, 140, 172
Reilly, Sir Charles 202
Reilly, Paul (later Lord Reilly) 73, 198, 201-3, 205, 206
Richard Shops 18, 184
Richards, JM 50
Richardson, Sir Albert 65
Ridgeway Hotel, Lusaka 46, 70
Rippon, Geoffrey 59
RMJM 92
Roche, Frederick Lloyd 107, 184, 187, 205
Rogers, Ruth 140
Ronson, Gerald 142, 181
Rose, Sir Francis 134
Rowlands, David 163, 169
Royal Academy 23
Royal College of Art (RCA) 19, 45, 59-60, 179, 209, 230
Royal Society of Arts 73
Ruscoe, William 33
Russell, Dick 76
Russell, Gordon 80
Russell, Ken 91
Russell, RD 152
Ryman 111, 112, 149, 152, 160
Ryman, Maurice 149

S
Saarinen, Eero 69, 161, 169
Saatchi brothers 107
Sainsbury 183
St Andrews Place residence 19, 140, 154, 168, 172
St John Wilson, Colin 50, 89
Sampe, Astrid 134
Sapper, Richard 183

Sargent, Sir Malcolm 74
SavaCentre 183
Scandinavia 113, 145
Scarpa, Carlo 145
Scherman, Betsy 120
Schottlander, Bernard 50
Science Museum 203, 205, 211
Scott, Peter 97, 101
Scott, William 52
Second World War 26-7, 44, 63-5, 79, 117-18
Seelig, Roger 149, 179-81, 184
Seibu department store 184
Sellers, Libby 210
Sempill, Cecilia 33
Serota, Nicholas 211, 216
Shaw, Norman 28, 31, 36
Shostak, Lee 187
Simpson department store, Piccadilly 17, 87, 90-1, 93, 127, 145
Sironi, Mario 201
Slade art school 29, 30, 41, 52
Sloane Court West Residence 89-91
Sloper (née Willis), Jane 25
Sloper, William 25
Sloper family 25, 26
Slutzky, Naum 38
Smith, Christina 55, 58-9, 137
Smith, Dick, Sun Curtain 60
Smith, Dodie 176
Smith, Paul 214
Smith, Richard 55, 120, 142, 169
Smithson, Alison 43, 44, 51, 52-3, 92, 148
Parallel of Life and Art 48, 50
Smithson, Peter 43, 44, 48, 50, 51, 52-3, 92, 148
Snowdon, Tony 149
Sochor, Zdenek 40
Soft Machine 58
Sony 157
Sottsass, Ettore 157, 203
Soukop, Willi 30
Soup Kitchen restaurants 87, 107, 119-20, 121, 124-5, 140-1
Southwark 187, 190
Sparke, Penny 203
Spence, Basil 76, 137
Spencer, Herbert 52
Spencer, Vera 52
Spry, Constance 68, 210
Stella, Frank 53, 55
Stephenson, John 107, 108
Stepney 26

INDEX

stereos 159, 170
Stirling, James 84, 187
Stokes, Anthony 59
Storehouse 18, 141, 149, 172, 175, 179, 181-4, 208, 227, 230
Storey, Ivan 87, 120, 124, 125
Strangeways, Christopher 203
Strong, Roy 203, 205, 206
Studio, The 134
Suez Canal 73
Sullivan, Olive 87-8
Summerly, Felix 198
Sunday Times, The (newspaper) 129, 145-6, 152-3, 157
Surrealism 49
Sutcliffe, Sean 13
Sutherland, Graham 83
Svensk Team store, Stockholm 145
Sweden 20, 142

T
Taste exhibition 206, 207
Tate Gallery 49, 71, 73, 201, 203, 205, 206, 211, 216
Tate Modern 190, 211
Taverne, Suzanna 216
Taylor, John 149
Taylor, Pagan 148, 149
television 81, 82
Thatcher, Margaret 18-19, 175, 178-9, 202, 208
Thetford factory, Norfolk 107, 110-11, 112, 114, 149, 152-3, 169, 202
This is Tomorrow exhibition 51, 52, 63, 149
Thomas, Mark Hartland 77
Thomas, Rodney 76, 77
Thompson, Ben 145
Thompson, Jane 145
Thompson, Paul 209
Tisdall, Hans 38
Tizio 183
Tomalin, Claire 129
Tomalin, Nick 129
Tomorrow's Future exhibition (1952) 50
Top Shop 180, 183
Tottenham Court Road 17, 23, 149, 154, 175-7, 202
toys 159-64
Triennale exhibitions, Milan 200, 201
Trieste hotel, Vienna 141
Triumph 63, 84, 108, 109

Tubbs, Ralph 75, 76, 77, 82
Turnbull, William 41

U
United States 20, 70, 73, 142
University of the Arts, London 38
'utility' designs 80

van der Rohe, Mies 53, 113, 172, 199, 216
Vertès, Marcel 120
Victoria and Albert Museum 36, 60, 65, 70, 82, 103, 193, 195-6, 197, 198-202, 205-6, 207, 209, 211, 216
Vogue magazine 108, 149

W
Wall Street 180-1
Wallace Collection 69-70
Wallpaper Manufacturers Ltd (WPM) 103
Ward, Neville 80
Ward, Reg 187-90
Warwick Gardens residence 87, 89, 120
Wegner, Hans 70, 145
welding 43, 46, 89, 92-3, 94, 230
White Cube 59
Whitechapel Gallery 51, 52, 63
Wickham, Julyan 190
Wickham, Michael 87-9, 121, 164, 190
Williams, Stanton 208
Willis, Lord Chief Justice Sir John 25
Wilmers, Mary-Kay 128-9
Wilson, Harold 65
Wilton, Ian 74
Winer, Charles 134
Wirth-Miller, Denis 179
WMP 96
Women's Voluntary Service 117
Woolland Brothers 107, 148-9
Wrecclesham commercial pottery 33

Z
Zilkha, Selim 179

243

Picture Credits

Every reasonable attempt has been made to identify owners of copyright. Errors and omissions notified to the publisher will be corrected in subsequent editions. Abbreviations are: R – right, L – left, T – top, B – bottom, C – centre, TR – top right, TL – top left, BR – bottom right, BL – bottom left.

Unless otherwise stated images are courtesy of Lady Conran on behalf of the Barton Court Estate.

Architectural Press Archive/RIBA Collections: p. 74r, 76, 78b, 82, 92, 112b; Architectural Review: p. 18; Ashley Havinden: p.194; Courtesy of Benchmark/Angus Thomas Photography: p.16br; Courtesy of Benchmark/Petr Krejci: 14-5; Bryanston School: p. 28, 31t, 31c; © Catherine Hyland: p. 9; Chris Ware/Stringer: p.74l; Courtesy of Conran & Partners: 136b, 137; Courtesy of Conran & Partners/Photo Ray Philips: p. 185t, 185bl; Courtesy of the Conran Shop: p. 228-9; The Design Council Slide Collection at Manchester Metropolitan University Special Collections: p. 19; D&D London: 138t, 139b; © David Hockney: p.56-7; David Pollack/Contributor: p. 35; David Soulsby/Alamy Stock Photo: p. 27; Design Council Archive, University of Brighton Design Archives: p. 81t, 81b, 91, 123t, 195l, 198; © the Design Museum: p. 20, 32, 101br, 186, 188-9, 202, 204, 207, 209, 212-3, 215tl; Express/Hulton Archive/Getty Images: p. 127; Gareth Gardner: p. 44, 219, 220-1, 222t; Geffrye Museum/Alamy Stock Photo: 101t; Heritage Image Partnership Ltd/Alamy Stock Photo: p. 78t; © Historic England Archive: p. 185br; © Hulton-Deutsch Collection/CORBIS/Corbis via Getty Images: p. 47t, 66, 75c; John Donat/RIBA Collections: p. 42-3; John Maltby/RIBA Collections: p. 107, 110, 111, 112t, 113, 114, 146l, 147, 155, 195r; Keystone/Hulton Archive/Getty Images: p. 31b; La Mediterranée: p. 120; Liam White/Alamy Stock Photo: p .203; © London Metropolitan Archives (City of London): p. 34; Luke Hayes: p. 214b, 215tr, 215b, 218, 222b, 223b; © Marcus Harrison/Bridgeman Images: 139t; Mark Blower: p. 223t; © Mark Boxer Estate: p. 128; Maurice Rougemont/Gamma-Rapho via Getty Images: p. 230; Michael Radford: p. 8t, 8b, 10-1, 12, 16t, 16bl, 33, 72, 101bl, 122, 132, 133, 156, 158, 160, 161, 162-3, 164, 165, 168, 169, 170, 171, 232-3; © Michael Wickham: p. 130, 131; © National Portrait Gallery, London/© the estate of W. Suschitzky: p. 77;

© Nigel Henderson Estate: Endpapers; © Nigel Henderson Estate/Tate Images: p. 41r, 47bl, 48b; PA Images/Alamy Stock Photo: p. 178, 201; Patricia Lyttelton: p. 121br; Peter Jordan/Alamy Stock Photo: p. 180r; Peter Scholey/Alamy Stock Photo: 136t; Picture Kitchen/Alamy Stock Photo: p. 118; Collection of Priscilla Carluccio: p. 24r; Private collection: p. 38; RIBA Collections: p. 64t, 64b, 123b, 125, 126, 176, 196; Smith Archive/Alamy Stock Photo: p. 53; © Tate Images: p. 39t, 41l, 51, 90t, 90b; © Terence Donovan/Camera Press: 150-1; Courtesy of The Fine Art Society; p. 94, 95; Tom Stoddart/Getty Images: p. 138b; Tony Kyriacou/Shutterstock: p. 214t; © Triennale Milano – Archivi: p. 200; Trinity Mirror/Mirrorpix/Alamy Stock Photo: p. 75t, 75b; © Victoria and Albert Museum, London: p. 110t, 110b, 197; Vivien Hislop: p. 121bl; Westminster Abbey Library: p. 37; Westwood/Popperfoto via Getty Images: p. 67.

Credits for the dust jacket and cover: © Ashley Havinden; Courtesy of Conran & Partners; Courtesy of Conran & Partners/Photo Ray Philips; Courtesy of the Conran Shop; Design Council Archive, University of Brighton Design Archives; © the Design Museum; Courtesy of The Fine Art Society; Gareth Gardner; John Maltby/RIBA Collections; © Julian Broad/National Portrait Gallery, London; Luke Hayes; Michael Radford; © Michael Wickham; © Nigel Henderson Estate/Tate Images; Patricia Lyttelton; Popperfoto via Getty Images/Getty Images; © Ray Williams; RIBA Collections; © Tate Images; © Terence Donovan/Camera Press; Westwood/Popperfoto via Getty Images.

Design Museum Publishing
Design Museum Enterprises Ltd
224–238 Kensington High Street
London W8 6AG
United Kingdom

designmuseum.org

First published in 2021
© 2021 Design Museum Publishing

ISBN 978-1-872005-59-1

All rights reserved. No part of this publication may be reproduced, stored in a retrieval system or transmitted, in any form by any means, electronic, mechanical, photocopying, recording or otherwise, without the prior permission of Design Museum Publishing.

Publishing Manager: Mark Cortes Favis

Picture Researcher: Anabel Navarro

Copyeditor: Liz Jones

Proofreader: Simon Coppock

Designer: Studio Fernando Gutiérrez

Artworker: Chris Benfield

Many thanks to Nu-Nu Yee Hoggarth for her patient help with realising this book, to Su Rogers and John Miller, in whose home in France much of it was written, and to Sarah Miller.

Many colleagues at the Design Museum have supported this book, and thanks go to them all.

Printed and bound in the UK by Pureprint